KYLE'S DEDICATION

This book has been a lot of fun for me. So often, once people see how their upbringing has affected them through the Inquiry Method process, they want to take it into their parenting. This shift requires a change in perspective.

This new perspective requires courage because it goes in the face of the most charged subject in our culture. Nothing brings out more self-righteousness than the subject of parenting.

The basic premise of the *Stop Parenting* philosophy is that if you are struggling, upset, bothered, disturbed, frustrated, judgmental, harsh, angry, sad, guilty, embarrassed, afraid, humiliated, defensive, overly protective, etc., it's not about your child, it's about you. You cannot be a good parent while you think your upset is about your child.

It's my hope that through this book you become willing and able to look at yourself and develop a new view of you, the process of creating an environment for a human being to become himself or herself, and of your child (and everyone else in your life).

This book is dedicated to Karen and Charlie: Karen for her courage to take a look at herself and walk through the fire of transformation, and Charlie for being such a good teacher for her. May you be so blessed.

-Kyle Mercer,
Ashland, Oregon

KAREN'S DEDICATION

For Kyle Mercer, whose insights have enriched my life immeasurably. Thank you for speaking to me in a register I could hear.

ACKNOWLEDGEMENTS

Books don't transform themselves from ideas into artifacts without the support of a tribe. I am filled with gratitude for the support of an ever-growing tribe of amazing people, parents and non-parents alike.

Stop Parenting got launched by the generosity of spirit of the participants of the May 2015 Mountain Experience. Early draft readers Isha Hadigan, Diane Hanfling Reed, Sally Kendall, and Jamie Hogue-Scelzi made valuable contributions to the content and tone of the manuscript. Seacrest Country Day School's teachers have accelerated my growth as much as my son's: Terry Dalton, Beverly Maranto, Terry Gardino, Erin Duffy, Katherine Arpin, and John Watson. Charlie's caregivers have been a steadfast source of wisdom, friendship and support, most especially Valerie Donovan and Carolina Villegas. The following medical professionals have become fierce advocates and true friends: Betsy Brothers, Jeffrey Ewig, Carol Golly, Magdalen Gondor, Deanna Green, Thomas Lahiri, Susan Nolan, Debra Shepard, and Viraine Weerasoriya. A few non-parent friends have been especially patient and insightful on the subject of parenting: John Argueso, Dean Davis, J. T. Jacoby, Lyn Millner, and Sydney Sorenson. I am profoundly grateful to you all.

Stop Parenting wouldn't exist without my small band of mommy compatriots. The following women have been truly amazing sounding boards, always available to share pain and laughter, and equally honest about their own adventures in parenting: Erin Almond, Mary Brandt, Linda Cashdan, Leslie Charlesworth, Patricia Cremin, Luisette Damiani, Karyn Everham, Linda Faillace, Julie Fanburg, Barbara Greenfield, Leslie Roffwarg, Barbara Rosenfeld, Chris Rosenman, Megan Stielstra, Judy Viorst, Mary Pelak Walch, Ruth Wenger, and Rae Healey-Young. Some righteous dads who have been equally open and inspiring about their parenting journeys are Steve Almond, Ed Freeman, Larry Faillace, Jonny Markowitz, and Aaron Roffwarg. Who rocks more than this band of parents? Nobody, that's who.

Now for my family. I thank Tom DeMarchi for creating a person with me and embarking on this crazy parenting ride even though he knew (better than I) that it would cost him the last of his youthful dark hair.

I thank Martin Tolchin for proving again and again that a parent's wellspring of love never comes close to running dry. Ditto a parent's sense of humor.

I lost my beloved mother, Susan Jane Tolchin, during the writing of this book. Her example of love—enduring, idiosyncratic, and true—will guide me always, along with that of my late brother Charlie. Losing you both made me stronger than I ever wanted to be.

Most of all, I thank Charlie Tolchin DeMarchi just for being my son. Eight years ago, you chose to jump off a cloud right into my arms, and my life is so much the richer for it. Know that you are strong and that you are loved. When you're all grown up, you might consider sending your Uncle Kyle a letter of thanks, perhaps with a really nice muffin basket. Or not; it's totally up to you.

-Karen R. Tolchin,
Naples, Florida

CONTENTS

STOP PARENTING

By Karen R. Tolchin, Ph.D. in conversation with Kyle Mercer

"I have found the best way to give advice to your children is to find out what they want and then advise them to do it."

-Harry S. Truman

INTRODUCTION

Twenty of us gather in a hotel conference room in Singer Island, Florida, mostly strangers who smile tentatively at each other as we check in with a young woman named Jamie. Jamie wears funky silver high heels and pale yellow pants that match her hair. Her eyes are a startling, Nordic blue. She hands out journals embossed with the words *Inquiry Method*. We peel off the cellophane and write our names inside the covers.

We're all poised to embark on a spiritual renewal retreat called "The Mountain Experience." Although we're 682 miles away from the nearest mountain (in Helen, Georgia), the title seems apt. The air crackles with the sort of energy that people must bring to Base Camp on Everest. A heavily tattooed man shifts from side to side, flashing me a warm but anxious smile. A young woman in yoga pants gnaws her thumbnail. I intuit that our weekend will involve some real personal risk, and that the strangers around me are beginning to realize the same thing. I've signed up because something tells me that the rewards of gaining some spiritual altitude will be worth it.

Outside our conference room, families in brightly colored swimsuits amble past our window. Parents are loaded down with pool noodles and beach totes, and their children race ahead, eager to test their mettle in the navy blue and turquoise surf. It's Mother's Day weekend, but I've left my child back home.

Only my guilt is portable.

We've gathered to learn from a man named Kyle Mercer. Five minutes with Kyle and it becomes clear that helping others is his true calling. He developed a practice called *Inquiry Method* and has been working as a professional life coach and running retreats like "The Mountain Experience" for twenty years. Approximately three thousand people have attended his seminars.

I've chosen to come to the Mountain Experience for lots of reasons. Despite all of my external markers of success—a meaningful career as a ranked college English professor, marriage with a fellow creative writer and professor named Tom, a beautiful six-year-old son named Charlie, a strong relationship with my parents, terrific friendships, financial security, etc.—I've been struggling mightily. In fact, this isn't the first time I've met Kyle in a hotel on Florida's east coast, despite the fact that neither of us lives here. I live in Naples, Florida, and he lives in Ashland, Oregon. We met nine months ago for an intensive private coaching weekend with my husband Tom, at the suggestion of my friend Diane, a longtime client of Kyle's who is now a life coach herself. "I just think you could be happier," Diane said to me. Since then, I've been having weekly coaching calls with him. After each one, I wonder how someone can divine so much about me and then provide so much relief from the side of a mountain on the opposite end of the United States.

Kyle makes his entrance and asks us to stand and form a circle. We prepare to receive our first gift from him. It's a gift none of us knows enough to want before we receive it.

"We're going to start by creating sanctuary," Kyle tells us. He asks us to agree to some basic ground rules for our weekend retreat, including that we refrain from drug use and agree not to divulge other people's secrets after we leave.[1] We all show him "Yes" by taking a step forward into the circle. Then Kyle gets quiet, and the barometric pressure in the room drops. In calming and centering himself, Kyle models the same way of being for us. We follow him into a deeper level of presence.

---

[1]   The authors have obtained permission to use the details included here.

Kyle is not a tall man, but he emanates a deep tranquility that makes him seem like a human Sequoia. His dark blue eyes tell me that he has weathered genuine sadness in his life, but also that he has felt plenty of joy. There's an intelligence and a soulful quality in those eyes, an unusually deep capacity for the acceptance of others. He must spend a fair amount of time walking in the woods in his hometown of Ashland, Oregon, given his tanned skin, his shaved head/ full beard combo, and the grounded, confident way he holds himself in his plaid shirt and jeans. Add to the mix Kyle's joyful, mischievous, and whole-hearted laughter, and you begin to get a sense of the man.

Kyle holds a Masters in Education that he is quick to disavow. He isn't heavily laden with diplomas and certifications. Instead, he is more of a modern-day shaman. He's acquired knowledge from a variety of sources, with a particular emphasis on the Indian Yogic tradition. He intuits the places in need of healing, new strategies, and wisdom. Then he gets to work.

Kyle makes his way slowly around the inside of our circle. He stands in front of each of us and holds our gaze for an extended moment.

"I want to be totally safe for you," he tells a thirty-one-year-old art teacher from Colorado.

"I won't hurt you in any way," he tells a silver-haired plastic surgeon from South Africa.

"I see you," he tells a former Air Force soldier who currently lives as the stay-at-home mom of toddlers in southeast Florida.

"You don't have to do anything to earn this," he tells a single pediatrician from Denver.

"I won't judge you in any way," he tells a construction worker from New Jersey. "I won't gossip about you, or talk about you behind your back."

"I just want to blow wind in your sails," he tells a retired dentist from New York.

"I promise not to rescue you," he tells a physician's assistant from Oregon who has come with his wife. "I know that you already have everything that you need."

"I'm just looking for the uniqueness and individuality of who you are," he tells a female small business owner from North Carolina. "You don't have to protect yourself. You don't have to defend."

By almost every available measure, everyone in the room is an American success story. We have love and friendship in our lives, we have families, we have homes, we have cars, we have earned advanced degrees, we have our health, we have meaningful work, we pursue various interests, and we give back to our communities. The majority of us have chosen professions that involve service to others. We are privileged in that we all have enough money, time, and support in our lives to attend this retreat and stay at this posh seaside resort. Yet by the time Kyle has completed his circle, half of us are crying. I watch the lovely pediatrician from Denver struggle to accept sanctuary from Kyle, her face turning dark red with emotion, and I find myself crying first for her and then for myself. When was the last time anyone ever provided total sanctuary for us, love without any conditions attached? Had we *ever* received this gift before? And how could something so basic and so nourishing be so rare?

One thing becomes clear: I wish everyone on earth could feel Kyle's brand of sanctuary, if only for a moment.

———

In the nine months since we first began talking, Kyle has been helping me shift my perspective on just about every front. In a recent coaching call, I tell him about a struggle I'm having with my son.

"Oh, I see what's going on," he says with a laugh. "Quit parenting."

"What?" I say. "You mean, like, give Charlie up for adoption? But I've grown kind of attached to him..."

"No, no, no," he says. "Just stop parenting."

Of all the ideas Kyle Mercer has thrown my way, this is by far the most radical. I'm parenting with all of my might, as if my life—and Charlie's—depends on it. "But 'parent' is a verb," I say. "Its synonyms are teach, mold, shape, instill, educate, protect, guide, and sacrifice." If I no longer approached parenting this way, wouldn't that make me a bad mother? Wouldn't Charlie suffer? How on earth could I *stop parenting*? How could that *possibly* be a good idea? What would that even *look* like?

Kyle piques my curiosity. I bring up another parenting struggle during a coaching call. Charlie's bedtime has become grueling for our whole family, a real horror show. It might have something to do with the fact that I co-slept with him for two years, or that I'm working too much during the day, or that Charlie is beginning to break a little under the strain of all the preventive medical treatment demands we place on him for a condition called cystic fibrosis. Then again, it might just be happening because he's six years old, and little kids resist bedtime. One night, he's pitching an epic fit—screaming, crying, scratching himself on the legs, and saying he hates himself. Tom and I grow alarmed.

I rush to soothe Charlie by holding him and telling him that he's a good boy and has a good heart. He wails in my arms. "How do you know I have a good heart?" he asks. I think about it for a minute, trying to imagine what all the experts call an "age appropriate" answer, and this is what I come up with: "Because Daddy and I made you, and we made your heart, and we put all the best things we could find in it, like rivers and mountains and puppies and rainbows and unicorns."

When I relate the story to Kyle, I hear a sharp intake of breath.

"What is it?" I say. How could an affirmation of the goodness of my son's heart be wrong?

"Charlie knows perfectly well that his heart isn't filled with rainbows and unicorns," Kyle says.

Kyle gives me additional feedback, but I can't hear another word. I'm too distressed. I had only meant to help my son. Have I instead done him some irreparable harm?

That night, I have trouble sleeping, and I'm still shaken the next day. I confide in two close friends over lunch. Before they weigh in, they pause and share a look, the sort of look that says, "Gee, I really hope our friend hasn't fallen in with some charismatic cult leader. We might have to stage an intervention before she becomes Wife #587 and starts selling daisies for him at the airport." These are friends who know that I am a natural embracer of new ideas, a seeker. They're aware that I have the skepticism of a trained academic, but still. They know the seeker in me beats out the skeptic every time—at least in the beginning.

"I *love* what you said to Charlie," the first friend says. "I wish my own mother had said something like that to me when I was young."

"I don't think I like your new life coach," says my other friend. "Who the heck is this Oregon mountain man, anyway, and what does he know about being a mother?"

I decide that I will heed all kinds of advice from Kyle, but that I'm going to put a sort of bracket around parenting.

"Kyle has a lot of good ideas," I tell Tom that night, "but his take on parenting feels too radical to me. I think we should take what he says about it with a grain of salt." Tom is on board, enthusiastically so.

"That's my philosophy about pretty much everything," he says.

We are nothing if not a study in contrasts.

After a few weeks, my resolve not to discuss parenting with Kyle erodes. My major struggles center on parenting. This is no surprise; after all, my entire life hinges on Charlie Jr.'s life. But I'm starting to get calm enough, open enough, and curious enough to hear what Kyle has to offer. What if there might be a better way to help Charlie when he's in distress, something more lasting than my swooping down to rescue him with unicorns and rainbows and BandAids? What if I could give him the tools to soothe his own troubled heart? Better still, what if I could heal my own troubled heart and then lead by example?

I don't know why anyone else has come to "The Mountain Experience" retreat, but my top reason for coming is to become a better parent. This is ironic because it's Mother's Day weekend and I've left my child home with Tom and a nanny in order to be here with a bunch of strangers.

Over the course of the weekend, it occurs to me that, despite all of the differences in our particular experiences, we all have one thing in common: We have never experienced deep acceptance and unconditional love, and this has marked us for trouble as adults. A couple of us had terrible, neglectful, or harmful parents, villains straight out of Dickens. Yet the majority of us—myself included—had parents who showed us in many ways that their love for us was profound and undeniable. If there had been a Hippocratic Oath for parents that began "First do no harm," all of our parents would have taken it freely, with an abundance of hope and love... *and still botched the job.*

What baffles me at the Mountain Experience is how even the most loving, dedicated parents, like mine, somehow failed to transmit the most basic things to their children, things Kyle is actively trying to transmit to us now. Like we *aren't* inherently broken or flawed people in need of shaping and molding. Like we *don't* have to prove our worth in this world over and over again through any particular action. Like we *already have inside of us* everything we need to heal ourselves. Worst of all is what *did* get transmitted, including a general sense of unease in the world, an inexhaustible wellspring of shame, a tendency to prize thinking over feeling, a Gordian knot of emotional entanglements, and a belief that a sense of duty (as opposed to what is true for us) should guide our daily choices.

Over the course of the weekend, I participate in several group and individual activities designed to help us free ourselves from decades of accumulated emotional pain and mistaken beliefs. I begin to reconnect with my deepest self, to feel the wide range of feelings that exists in all of us without shame, and to trust in my inner knowing.

"I want to be rid of my fears," I tell Kyle in front of the whole group. I list my phobias, a short but potent list headlined by germophobia, and I hear murmurs of appreciation from the group. These people know it's not easy to make it through the day when you see a mine-field of potential catastrophes.

"Your fears all seem to fall under the heading of 'struggle with life'," Kyle says, and the truth of his assessment staggers me. I have been struggling to control every aspect of my world, with almost no success—to Purell away every threat to my child's health, to replace every one of his psychological pains with a unicorn. Would it be possible to give up that struggle without harming Charlie or myself? Was my hyper vigilance helping anyone at all, or was it the biggest source of actual damage in my household?

As a parent who is *uber*-focused on getting it right, I grow more and more alarmed by the scope of damage even the best parents have done to the good people of this retreat. Excluding one or two participants who were abandoned as children and/or parented by deeply troubled people, we all had parents who bought into our culture's most highly touted values.

As I'm listening, I begin to sketch a Top Ten list of widely-held beliefs about parenting in our culture. Here's how it takes shape:

1. Being a parent is the most important job you will ever have, so you should do it as if your life and the lives of your children depend on it;

2. Good parents are inextricably tied to their children on an emotional level;

3. Parents ought to tell their children what kind of behavior works and doesn't work out in the world, because the world depends on parents to teach children how to behave;

4. Left to their own devices, children will run amok; Good parents exert control over their kids, while bad children resist that control;

5. Children don't know what's best for them, so parents should actively correct, mold, shape, and choose for their children;

6. The world is full of dangers, and protecting children from them should be a top priority;

7. Parents should foster their children's self esteem with lots of praise, and they should rush to intervene when their children feel bad;

8. Parents should instill in their children a sense of respect, duty, and family obligation. Children should put duty to family above personal instincts;

9. It's possible to parent well no matter what physical/emotional shape you might be in yourself. In fact, being exhausted, overweight, and stressed out is probably a sign that you are a selfless, i.e. good parent, who puts your children's needs before your own; and

10. To see how well or how poorly someone has performed as a mom or dad, just look at the child. The child is a walking report card for the parent.

When I got pregnant, I subscribed to *every single one* of these beliefs. I approached motherhood with the focus and diligence of an Olympian. I gave myself over seven hundred hypodermic needles to the stomach during my fertility treatments, (an atypical sacrifice necessitated by a blood clotting disorder). I rubbed oil on my skin and sang, "You are My Sunshine" to my bump every single day of my pregnancy. I lost entire days to the reality TV series "A Baby Story."

Because I am and always will be a bookish creature, I pored over parenting manuals and books and memoirs and meditations, starting with Alexander Tsiaras's gorgeously curated photography book *From Conception to Birth* (2002).

"The baby is the size of a lentil," I told my extended family. The next week, "The baby is a lima bean." I counted myself grateful to have cutting edge, 21st century wisdom to cull for all the very best practices on how to feed, clothe, discipline, educate, praise, and otherwise manifest an amazing life for my child. When my friend Beth Ann Fennelly gave me a copy of her own book, *Great With Child: Letters To a Young Mother*, I gulped it down and quickly got drunk on its power and beauty. I sympathized with Amy Chua's high hopes for her children and her befuddlement at their resistance to her controlling impulses in *The Battle Hymn of the Tiger Mother*. (I also marveled at Chua's stamina, working full-time as a Yale law professor and still attending all of her daughters' music lessons with them.) Andrew Solomon's *Far From the Tree: Parents, Children, and the Search for Identity* terrified me in much the same way as *What To Expect When You're Expecting*—two *Worst Case Scenario Handbooks* come to life. Solomon examines the lives of parents who gave life to children wholly different from themselves, often with severe disabilities, and then struggled mightily to accept those differences. As for *What to Expect*… well, it can make a woman like me suspect that her unborn child might have a rare disorder commonly found in water fowl.

As far as parenting philosophies and guides go, I was easily won over by the wisdom of *The Baby Book: Everything You Need to Know About Your Baby from Birth to Age Two* (1993) by pediatrician William Sears and his wife Martha, a registered nurse. Sears is known as the Father of Attachment Parenting, a recent approach that grew out of Attachment Theory in psychology. Sears advocates a return to a more connected, aboriginal ethos. One of my mommy friends explained it to me as a corrective to the 20th century's cold take on parenting. She summarized it as follows: "People used to put babies in cribs down the hall, behind bars, like hardened criminals. You're born, and then you're cast out in the cold, with a bottle full of toxic formula, Ferberized and left to cry. How barbaric can you get?" I shuddered and distinctly had this thought: "Not my child." No child of mine would suffer like that, not while I could feed him the perfect food of my breastmilk, share my bed with him at night, and wear him in a Baby Bjorn during the day. Why get in the parenting business just to reject and damage someone?

I had the zeal of the new convert.

My 20th century mother began to give me worried looks. She loved to tell the story about being flat on her back after a C-section when the La Leche League paid her a visit. "I sent them packing!" She was proud of her non-attachment. To be fair, the breast pump circa 1970 must have seemed about as portable and user-friendly as a nuclear reactor.

"You slept in a crib and were bottle-fed, and you turned out just fine," she said.

Define "fine."

By breathtaking contrast, Tom was about a thousand times more relaxed about Project Baby. He didn't read a single book about parenting while I was pregnant. At various points, he suggested lots of imaginative ideas, the most outlandish of which was that I deliver our baby in the swimming pool... and then raise him in it so he could keep the ability to breathe in a watery environment.

Six years later, I believe Tom still hasn't cracked a single parenting book, no matter how many I highlight and leave open at choice passages around our home. He has a radically different process, one that involves listening to a lot of Elvis Costello. I try not to judge, especially since he's experiencing parenthood in a much calmer way.

Meanwhile, I grow more and more obsessed with gaining knowledge that might help us all thrive. I want more than anything else in life to be a good mother.

Once Charlie arrives, I see that motherhood is going to be much harder than I expected, and that the stakes are exponentially higher. The new love I feel for my son makes my worst romantic crushes seem as inconsequential as mosquito bites.

From my new vantage point as a parent, my friend Jennifer Senior's *All Joy and No Fun: The Paradox of Modern Parenting* is by far the best book I have encountered. In a radical departure, she investigates the effects of contemporary parenting styles not on the children but rather on their parents. Her book depicts an epidemic of exhausted, frustrated mothers with lots of tension in their marriages, and narcissistic children accustomed to continuous attention. Her wise, funny, and accurate account makes me doubly grateful to call her my friend.

While I'll never regret nursing my son when he was an infant, or co-sleeping with him for the first two years of his life, or wearing him in a baby carrier as much as I could,

or striving to make him feel safe and loved in this world—all basic tenets of contemporary Attachment Parenting—I immediately recognize myself, my marriage, and aspects of my child's behavior in the *All Joy* portrait.

Jennifer demonstrates that our parenting culture might be more than a little off kilter, but *All Joy, No Fun* is more of a social history/cultural critique than a road map for struggling parents. I'm hungry for solutions.

Could Kyle's "Stop Parenting" approach be the solution for me? More to the point, am I—the fretful, intensely loving mom of a child with chronic medical needs—constitutionally capable of reinventing myself in such a radically new form?

At the Mountain Experience, we talk about what it might feel like to show up in the world feeling whole as opposed to damaged or victimized, and to design our lives around something other than a sense of obligation. We learn how to use Inquiry

Method with ourselves and others to bring more clarity, love, joy, and wisdom to our

lives and relationships. We are actually learning how to re-parent ourselves from a place of deep, eternal acceptance and sanctuary. I begin to feel lighter and more hopeful than I can remember.

"If I can model this way of being in the world for Charlie," I think, "maybe he won't need to attend a healing retreat like this one when he's a man."

This begins to seem possible, natural, and even easy until I'm forced to see how much I would need to change—practically on a cellular level—in order to stop parenting. I might as well be asking, "Can an apple become an orange?"

On the last night of the retreat, I have dinner alone with Kyle and Jamie, who is training to be an Inquiry Method coach. I am abuzz with all of the powerful lessons of the weekend. Yet as we make our way back to the hotel, I discover that many of my parenting beliefs remain as entrenched as ever. My cell phone vibrates and I look at it right away. It's a photo of Charlie at the helm of a boat. I show it to Kyle and Jamie.

"I hope that Charlie loves boating so much that he eventually wants to do something like a Semester at Sea!" I say. "It would be so great for him."

Both Kyle and Jamie look concerned.

"Wait—what'd I say?" I say, and they both laugh in a kind way.

"Maybe *you* want to do a semester at sea," Jamie gently suggests.

A little while later, it happens again when I tell Jamie and Kyle that I need to leave the retreat a few hours early the following day.

"If I'm away from Charlie for too long," I explain, "my heart hurts."

"Please make a note of that for our next coaching session," Kyle says. "We need to clean that up as soon as possible."

"But if my heart hurts when I'm away from my son," I ask, "isn't that appropriate? Just a sign that my love for my child is great?"

The short answer is "No." To sum up, in the school of Inquiry Method, I'm still just a freshman registering for classes.

───────────────

This book represents a series of conversations between a rank beginner and her wise and original life coach. I try to figure out how and why to stop parenting. I struggle mightily with Kyle Mercer's radical approach to the most typical parent-child interactions, relearning things as basic as how to talk to my own child about his day. I learn why the sentence "I have high hopes for my child" needs to go the way of the dodo bird. Is it possible for me to shift from a parent locked in action-verb-mode to a parent who sees parenthood as a calm, peaceful state of being? Can I "First do no harm"? Can someone who has been running her own classroom for two decades learn to shut up, stop teaching, and learn something new? Can I trade emotional entanglement for meaningful engagement? To sum up, can I stop parenting for the good of my entire family?

Can *you*?

Note: The following conversations cover a period when my son ranged in age from five to seven years old. We default to the masculine pronoun, not as a political statement but rather because we're talking about a boy.

Adam, Eve, and the Genesis of Stop Parenting

I t feels weirdly exhilarating to shift into professional mode with my life coach as we begin the process of writing this book together. In a short period of time, Kyle's become very important to me. I've cried with him, I've revealed my deepest sources of shame and suffering, and he has seen me at my pettiest, most fearful and bloated worst. By comparison, he's been funny and wise, the living embodiment of the concept "true north." To be sure, I'm in the full flower of analytical transference, but my respect for him is no trick.

At first, I'm excited to show him my literary skill set in action, but I quickly realize my mistake.

"Look, I'm not a complete waste of a human being!" I might as well be saying. "I can be very useful! I can be good! Love me and give me praise. Give me a gold star."

I'm talking with a life coach in large part to change that whole exhausting, misguided impulse. I want to dismantle that software and run a new program altogether. That's why I've chosen a life coach who isn't impressed by gold stars. No shaman worth his salt cares about diplomas.

When the exhilaration evaporates, I'm left with my old standby: worry. I grow more and more nervous about revealing the extent of my ignorance about what really matters, the subject of our book. How could someone who can't seem to stop parenting for even fifteen minutes hope to co-author a book called **Stop Parenting**?

One thing that may not translate onto the written page is the compassion that emanates from Kyle during our conversations. While his words sometimes feel harsh to me—along with the medicine being prescribed—Kyle's demeanor never is.

Karen Tolchin:	Could we start with a definition of the Inquiry Method? How did you develop it?
Kyle Mercer:	The Inquiry Method grew out of my desire to make a difference with people. When I was young I had a lot of ideas, but when I shared them, I found that people resisted. I ended up asking more and more questions. Through my questioning, I found that people were having deep insights and deep discovery. I use that process as a coach and as a teacher, to help my clients find a much deeper self-discovery, self-expression, self-understanding, and self-knowledge.
Karen Tolchin:	So the Inquiry Method is a coaching method intended to help people acquire knowledge for themselves.
Kyle Mercer:	That's right. But to do that, you need to clear up a lot of faulty beliefs. Gaining knowledge is often more about *unlearning* than learning.

Unlearning can be harder than learning.

Karen Tolchin: I've seen that firsthand so many times in my work as a teacher—how it can really be about helping people *unlearn* the wrong stuff first.

Once, way back when I was in grad school, I tutored the sweetest young woman, a very hard-working, diligent, Korean student. She had been taught to pronounce the silent "E." It would come across like "Home-y, home-y on the range-y."

Kyle Mercer: Not good!

Karen Tolchin: She had spent *years* back home practicing the wrong way. Getting her to grasp that single fact— that the silent "E" is supposed to be silent—took an entire semester of private tutoring. Over *sixteen weeks*, that's all we accomplished.

Kyle Mercer: I believe it. The lessons that we need to *unlearn* can be much harder than simply learning something new, because we just get bombarded with the wrong stuff. We absorb so much culturally, on so many levels, and from our parents, and all these external sources. Everybody's trying to teach us, shape us up, get us to conform and do it right, on all these different levels. It's a huge burden on each of us to try to maintain all the different levels and aspects, expectations, thoughts and beliefs, ideas.

Karen Tolchin: What do you mean, "we're all trying to maintain all the different levels and aspects"?

Kyle Mercer: Let's just look at the topic of parenting. How many different ideas are there about how to parent our children? Even within a partnership, a marriage, the couple can have all sorts of different ideas. It can create a lot of conflict.

Karen Tolchin: I'm definitely experiencing that right now with Tom. We seemed to have so much more in common *before* we had Charlie, or at least we thought we did. Now, on our worst days, we look at each other as if to say, "Who *are* you, and how did you get in my house? Please go away."

Kyle Mercer: Different perspectives emerge on hundreds of topics. Should we let our baby cry in the crib? What kind of education is right for our children? Are we spoiling them?

The best parenting comes from a deep peace, calm, and presence, along with the lightest touch.

Are we loving them enough? When do we hold them? When do we nurture them? When do we correct them? So many ideas about parenting are foisted upon us that we never, ever get a chance to tap into what's true for ourselves.

Our culture is so alive with ideas and thoughts about these things, we never actually get to make our own discoveries. We're too busy trying to do it "right."

Karen Tolchin: I certainly feel that pressure. Most of the moms I know are buckling under it, actually. It's "systems overload," so much noise. It's hard to figure out what's true.

Kyle Mercer: It really helps if you can quiet all the noise. That voice within is subtle and quiet. It takes some practice to hear it. With parenting, and with so much else in life, really, there's *so much less* to be done than we think. The chaos and all the competing thoughts in our mind keep us in this constantly agitated state.

The best parenting perspective is just a deep peace, calm, and presence, along with the lightest touch.

Karen Tolchin: "Just a deep peace, calm, and presence, along with the lightest touch." This is such a beautiful vision for how to move through the world as a parent! But how do we achieve it when our daily reality is a lot less beautiful, and a lot more chaotic? I know we're creating a lot of that chaos, but still…

By the way, I think that doing less, as a parent, is going to be my toughest challenge.

Kyle Mercer: Unquestionably, it will be. What I find is, the more we practice Inquiry Method, the more we let go of all these cultural ideas and expectations, and then there's a deep knowing and understanding that comes from inside. The fundamental knowledge that we need as human beings comes from two sources: from within ourselves, and from our direct experience with the world.

It's a totally flawed idea
that we're born flawed.

A big part of this **Stop Parenting** idea is to allow the inner nature of the individual to come through and be expressed. Most parents look at a child and say, "How am I going to whip him into shape?"

This idea that we're born, and we're very much flawed, and we need to be shaped up and developed into people who work, and that our parents are the ones who need to do the shaping—it's a totally flawed idea.

Karen Tolchin: So people are *not* born flawed and sinful, and in need of a massive overhaul?

Kyle Mercer: No. We're not. That's no longer so much a religious idea as a cultural one—that we're bad to the core. It transcends religion, and it's simply not true. We naturally want to be loving, engaged people. The most dysfunctional parts of human beings come out in environments that stimulate those responses.

Karen Tolchin: As a personal aside, I can see that very clearly after twenty years in Academe. Department meetings often stimulate the most dysfunctional parts of us. By contrast, our own classrooms bring out the best in us, which is why so many of us choose to stay and endure the politics.

Kyle Mercer: These dysfunctional beliefs are deeply ingrained in work culture, family culture, just everywhere. They're harmful.

When we toss out the belief that everyone is born bad to the core, and we assume that people are perfect the way that they're made, then we ask ourselves, "How do we allow that perfection to melt in and integrate with other people and society and culture?" From the parental role, there's nothing to be done except to love that individual.

Karen Tolchin: When I was pregnant, my parenting "To Do" list was hundreds of items long. "Just love him" would have streamlined matters enormously.

Kyle Mercer: That's right. On the other hand, we recognize that children need some socialization and culturalization. But here's the kicker: It's damaging for the parent to be the one that does the socialization. What's really healthy is giving that child the encouragement, the deep love, and the confidence to explore out into the world, and then to let their interaction with the world let them know what works or doesn't work. That's the only way they come to a real, authentic understanding.

The whole message of this modern era of parenting is to override who somebody is.

Karen Tolchin: I think I'm getting lost in the abstractions here. What's a concrete example of a belief-level idea that just doesn't work in the world?

Kyle Mercer: Well, a common parenting model is that we're supposed to please other people. "Share your toys even if you don't want to, share your candy even if you don't want to." What's being taught is that we're supposed to be nice to other people even when we don't feel it. So, all of a sudden this becomes an oppressive idea that somebody carries for a lifetime, because I'm supposed to be nice even when I don't feel it.

I would say that if we unlearn that belief, we could speak about our feelings in a way that could help resolve them. Or else, we could directly learn that when we choose to share our toys, people appreciate it. But we'd be choosing to do it authentically, in that case. When we over-lay this external idea over what we're actually feeling, it starts to create this heart/mind split.

Karen Tolchin: I can relate to that personally—the heart/mind split. Feeling a certain way, but forcing myself because of some thought, or expectation, to ignore my feelings.

Kyle Mercer: We've *all* been taught to do this. It's so profound. Almost all of us have gotten the idea that we are supposed to trust our minds and not our hearts—our thoughts, not our feelings. I don't mean nec-essarily emotional feelings, or surface reactions, but our deeper inner-knowing. I'm talking about that quiet voice within. We have to get rid of the thoughts and clean up the emotions to tap into that inner source.

I'm hoping that this book and others like it give rise to a new generation of people whose lives are rooted in what's true and natural rather than ideas that are supposed to override who we are. The whole message of this modern era of parenting is to override who somebody is. You have to modify yourself to be okay in the world, rather than explore yourself and find out what's true in you, and just be that truth.

Karen Tolchin: So that's what children *don't* need—to be trampled and modified. What *do* they need?

We're all starving for a different way of being.

Kyle Mercer: Direct experience. If we can replace indoctrination with really direct experience, then we're operating in a whole different manner. Then, whatever that child does, how he operates in the world, comes from a direct relationship to what's true in the world. That's just so much more powerful. When somebody has that inner confidence, that inner knowledge, that real experience of the world and applies it, he comes away with a whole different confidence.

Karen Tolchin: I love this vision, Kyle, but I honestly don't know a *single* person who was raised that way. That became so clear at the Mountain Experience— that *nobody* was raised with deep acceptance at home, and non-interference by parents.

Kyle Mercer: We're a whole culture of people trying to use ideas and thoughts to manage and operate. They just don't work. We're all in our heads rather than in an organic engagement, an organic way of seeing the world.

Karen Tolchin: Hey, we've finally recognized as a culture that our food and clothing should be organic. Maybe we're ready to see that our parenting should be organic, too.

Kyle Mercer: We're all starving for a different way of being, and dying for it. We worry that if we trust a more natural, authentic, organic way of being in the world, then our kids are going to be out of control, people are going to be out of control. We can't trust it. That's all a big part of this context that we've all been given.

Karen Tolchin: I'm lost again. What's the context we've been given?

Kyle Mercer: That you can't trust yourself. That you should trust the ideas that you've been given over yourself. This is classic. You trust the beliefs you're given, you trust the culture you're given, the ideas, the concepts, the orientation that you're given. It's all about trusting an abstraction. We're asked to trust all of these abstractions rather than having a direct experience of what works or doesn't work out in the world.

My father was abandoned and fended for himself at a very early age, which is part of the reason why he was able to teach me and other people a different way of viewing the world. He operated alone in the world, and no one interfered with him. He was allowed to have direct experience of the world, and it gave him deep street smarts. Street smarts are the same thing as what I am talking about, it just doesn't have to be in the streets.

The most destructive idea in western culture is that it's the parent's job to turn the child into something.

	It's a direct understanding of how the world works rather than trying to use ideas and beliefs.
Karen Tolchin:	I understand the value of street smarts, but I'm still a little unclear about all of these beliefs that don't serve us well. Could I have another example?
Kyle Mercer:	Okay, here's one. We're told that if we play fair, other people will play fair. Is that always true?
Karen Tolchin:	Definitely not. Again, I've had to learn that lesson over and over in Academe.
Kyle Mercer:	It happens time and time again with these ideas out in the world. Beliefs that we're taught, "If you do this, this will happen." If you're a good boy or a good girl, life will work for you. Life doesn't work like that.
Karen Tolchin:	So the alternative is cultivating a more organic way of being in the world—of having direct experiences, and adapting your behavior based on what you discover for yourself to be true.
Kyle Mercer:	That's right. Now, as for the *inorganic* way of being—I get caught in it, you get caught in it,

everybody gets caught in it. It's being in our heads rather than just being right here, present with this inner-knowing aspect that just engages with the world. Our minds are here for a specific purpose, but they've been twisted and used for a purpose that's really not appropriate.

Karen Tolchin: What do you mean? How do our minds get twisted?

Kyle Mercer: In Inquiry Method, sometimes we look at the individual in three different aspects. You can say Mind, Body, and Source, or you can say Mind, Emotions, and Source. (I put Emotions in the Body category.)

Mind is not there to be the leader, and yet we treat it as the leader. It's there to be a resource for that inner knowing part of ourselves. Mind is there to serve, not to be the master.

Stop Parenting puts the heart over the mind.

We don't want Emotion or Body to be the leader because we don't want to lead the way with anger, we don't want to lead the way with fear, or really with any emotion.

The master is supposed to be our own Source, or deep inner knowing. Source should be the leader, informed by Body/Emotions and executed by Mind.

Karen Tolchin:	Are we putting Mind before everything else? Maybe we should blame the Enlightenment.
Kyle Mercer:	Yes, we put Mind first. It's the whole flavor of modern parenting. "Think about what you just did. Why did you do that? Give me a rationale for why you did that. Think about what you did. I'll give you something to think about."
Karen Tolchin:	Yikes! I hadn't realized that before about the supremacy of Mind in parenting. It's deeply embedded in our language.
Kyle Mercer:	It's so direct. Now just imagine for a moment if we could create an environment where our children didn't get this brain disease, brain damage, really—i.e., that the mind is supposed to matter more than everything else, including your inner knowing. They would have this tremendous natural capacity and it would be unfettered.
Karen Tolchin:	Yet instead we choose to handicap our children by loading them up with crazy ideas and external rules? And we tell them it's for their own good.
Kyle Mercer:	That's right. Sure, we all need to understand and get the rules for being in the world, and how to interact. But as parents we don't have to foist them on our children. The rules for being in the world will come naturally to each of us, just because we don't want to be rejected. We all want to be effective, so we will adapt if what we're doing doesn't work. But if the message comes from the parents, it breaks this idea of just being totally loved exactly the way you are.
Karen Tolchin:	And that's a terrible loss. It's strange how few people seem to operate from a place of deep

security and a feeling of just being totally loved. I saw this so clearly at the Mountain Experience.

The parental source loves us just the way we are.

Kyle Mercer: That's right. We all need one source, which is the parental source, loving us just the way we are, so that we always have that as a grounding. Then we go out in the world to deal with all different kinds of people. We learn to interact with them, but we always come back to this source of unconditional love.

Karen Tolchin: I know that the Inquiry Method isn't a religion, but I really want to say "Amen." I'd love for every child in the world to feel this, for every person to feel this. I believe it would solve so many problems in our world.

Kyle Mercer: Amen.

"The Good Mother" and Other Sticks We Use to Beat Ourselves With

As someone who has been gunning for straight A's for what feels like a hundred years, first as a student and now as a college professor, I've evolved into someone whose most prominent characteristic appears to be earnestness. I'm dismayed to realize this, as I always wanted to be the sort of person who leads with passion or love or fearlessness or humor. Not something as needy as earnestness. But there's no denying it: I want so badly to get it right, as a person, as a wife, and most of all as a mother, that I'm consumed with good intentions, buzzing with intensity.

At the same time, I'm beginning to recognize the faulty logic that underpins my drive. What does it mean to get it right, anyway? I'm beginning to see that if I don't redouble my efforts to do my own spiritual work, to get calm and grounded, then the ways I've been twisted will yield an ugly harvest in my child.

In this conversation, Kyle debunks the myth of "The Good Mother" and other incarnations of parental guilt.

Karen Tolchin: So, it's beginning to dawn on me that your approach to parenting is exactly the opposite of what I've been taught, and what many of my parenting books say, so this is very counter-intuitive for me. At the same time, I can really feel

	the wisdom in it. I suspect this will be an antidote to the conventional wisdom that many other parents might appreciate as well.
Kyle Mercer:	Wonderful.
Karen Tolchin:	As a relatively new parent, I can see where the best intentions to be a source of deep love and acceptance can go haywire, and the expression of parent-to-child love can get conditional, and horribly twisted. You want to love your child unconditionally, but then you get all of these messages from the culture, and so you get busy shaping and molding...
Kyle Mercer:	I think that's well put. But when we say, "Be a source of unconditional love for your children," we want to get really clear about what that means. It's not gushy, adoring, fawning love, it's not sexual love, it's not romantic love. What I really mean is deep, unconditional acceptance. Deep unconditional acceptance means, "I totally accept this individual just the way that he is. I totally want to offer him his own unique expression and experience of life. My intention is not to interfere with that."

Rampant overparenting is creating narcissistic, self-important children.

I recognize that there are a great many things that interfere with this. A lot of it has to do with the ego and beliefs we have about parenting. Parental guilt is one of the most damaging effects of our ego that totally interferes with parenting.

Karen Tolchin: My child is only six years old, but I'm already an expert in parental guilt. I totally recognized myself in the portrait of all of the haggard mothers in Jennifer Senior's book *All Joy, No Fun: The Paradox of Modern Parenting*. I'm building a whole life around my child, exhausting myself to make sure his life is perfect, fretting about all of the ways I might be failing him, wrecking my marriage…

Kyle Mercer: It's rampant in our culture, these beliefs about parenting, about overparenting, about how important the children are. It's just creating extremely narcissistic, self-important children who are not responsible for themselves and stay dependent on other people long into adulthood.

This deep, unconditional love I'm talking about cultivating is *not* about a co-dependent enabling of dysfunctional behavior. This love is total acceptance, it's, "I'm a place that you can always come for safety, to be held, to be seen, to be known that you're just fine exactly the way you are." It doesn't mean that I'm going to create a dependency. You're still totally responsible for your own well-being. If a child within this context comes up and wants me to fix things, I'm there to support him in his own success. Not to hijack that and make it *my* success. The goal is always to support them in *his* success.

Karen Tolchin: I really want this for my child, and I want this for myself.

17

Kyle Mercer:	For us, who haven't been raised this way, who don't live in a culture that supports this, it's a very nuanced practice. If we didn't have our minds poisoned with all of these belief systems about parenting, it would come very easy and naturally, it would just be a matter of fact. Because our minds are so active about this, it takes a really special kind of self-discipline to be able to relate to our children in this way.
Karen Tolchin:	Jennifer Senior discovers that it's mostly mothers who are making ourselves crazy with this hyper-attentive parenting. I hate to admit it, but we mothers seem to be the ones who have swallowed whole some bill of goods. That if our kids are not in every extra-curricular activity, and they're not 100% the center of our being, then we're not good mothers.

The most difficult issue that I have to work through with women is the judgment on themselves as bad mothers.

If we're not good mothers, we're not good people. Her book is a portrait of exhausted, terrified women.

The guys, the fathers, are a little bit better at detaching. A little better at saying, "Okay, there's my time with my kid, and then there's my time with me." A little bit better at creating those ego

	boundaries. But that has created a huge amount of tension in marriages because mothers are saying, "Why am I so exhausted, while you look well-rested and happy?" I really think it all stems from what you're describing: this mentality that the child has to be the absolute end-all, be-all.
Kyle Mercer:	Let me jump in for a second, because I agree to a certain extent, and then I also want to give a caveat to that. When the women are that overly attached to the children, it frees the men not to worry so much about it. I've seen a lot of times that when the women back off, then the men start to get concerned and step forward.
	The second aspect that I think we also want to point out is that although men may be more detached in a positive sense, they're also not recognizing their role and responsibility in parenting. Now we're getting young boys who aren't learning how to be men, young women that aren't understanding the relationship with the masculine… Children are getting strange ideas because fathers are so detached that they feel abandoned.
	My point is that it's actually a universal dysfunction. It's not just limited to the women. Both parental roles are compromised by this contemporary approach.
Karen Tolchin:	That's a bit of a relief. It doesn't all fall on the moms. Speaking of moms, could you tell me what you think about the concept of the "Good Mother"?
Kyle Mercer:	Okay, great. Let's see if I can tap into that. I think the place to start is "Bad Mother."

19

Karen Tolchin: Great. "Bad Mother." I know they're only words, but boy, do they make me shiver.

If you think your parenting will shape your child's personality, how do you explain the radical differences between children in the same family?

Kyle Mercer: You and every mother I know. That's the problem.

We need to go back, I think, to something even more primal or basic. I think we have to go back to the first idea, the first cultural idea that interferes or informs all of this: That it's our job to turn the child into something. As parents, we're supposed to form and make the child out of clay, as if we were gods. To make them into a decent person. This is the most destructive idea in western culture. It's just so damaging in so many ways. One, it tells the child he's fundamentally not okay, that he needs to be fixed or repaired. Just by implication, by behavior, by thought, by pattern, just energetically even—children get this idea that they're just not okay. The adults that I work with are all struggling with this sense that there's something fundamentally wrong with them.

Karen Tolchin: It's mind-boggling to me, especially after the Mountain, to see that even those of us with

20

loving, devoted parents somehow failed to receive the message that we are fine just as we are.

Kyle Mercer: That's right. Now, as a parent, if I believe that it is my job to form my child into something, then the value of my parenting—how I parent, just in a linear way, as we do everything else in our culture—is seen in the outcome.

This is just insanity. I mean, you look at different kids in the same family and they'll turn out totally differently. With totally different outcomes.

Karen Tolchin: That's so true. I don't know any siblings who resemble each other except in the most superficial ways, not even twins.

Kyle Mercer: The fact that we act as if every outcome of every child within a family is a direct result of the parenting we have done is completely insane.

Some parents try to take credit. When their children go to Harvard, they say, "Look, I did this," which is a total lie. On the other hand, when their kid is in juvenile detention, they still feel guilty and terrible, as if it all comes down to something they did or did not do as parents. Equally wrong.

Parental guilt comes directly from the idea that we're responsible for the outcomes of our child's life.

Karen Tolchin:	Wait, so neither one of those things is true? As a parent, you can't take any of the credit for Harvard, or any of the blame for prison?
Kyle Mercer:	Exactly. Because your child is a person. He's not you.
Karen Tolchin:	I think this is going to be very hard for a lot of parents to swallow, and when I mean a lot of parents, I mean me.
Kyle Mercer:	The child is a person, not an object, and he or she has got his own life. That's the fundamental problem. As soon as we start taking credit, good or bad, for what this person does, now all of a sudden we're running up and down with their survival and their well-being, and seeing it as a reflection on us. It's like our child is an advertisement to the whole world.
Karen Tolchin:	That's the exhausted Jennifer Senior mom portrait all over again. We're all "running up and down" with our kids' survival. That's extra true for me as the mom of a child with a chronic medical condition.
Kyle Mercer:	That's right. Now, if you're my child, and I'm your mother, and you're having a bad day, and I'm like, "Oh, that's terrible, I did that," and now I'm fawning over you or trying to fix it, you learn that you aren't responsible for your own life. Maybe the father agrees, and is like, "Oh, I didn't have anything to with that," it wasn't the father's fault or something. So maybe I quit loving that kid. All because that kid just screwed up or whatever. It's total blindness on all sides.
Karen Tolchin:	Yipes. That's a nightmarish scenario, for sure.

22

Kyle Mercer: So parental guilt comes directly from the idea that we're responsible for the outcomes of that child's life. Then, we create this huge dependency, because we teach it to the children. They grow terrible parental resentment, because when their life isn't going the way they hoped it would, they go back and they blame it on their parents, rather than taking responsibility for it personally.

Karen Tolchin: It's just nightmares heaped upon nightmares.

Kyle Mercer: And fixing it! If you're my parent and I'm having a hard time, and you've taught me that it's your fault, even subconsciously, now I'm not going to take action. I'll see myself as a victim of your parenting, rather than as a person who has the power to change and manifest my life in any way I want.

Most of us are carrying around negative energy stemming from the belief that we're a victim of the parenting we received.

The more you start to look into it, you see what a disaster the whole thing is.

Karen Tolchin: What's especially tragic about this is that most parents just want their kids to be able to manifest happy lives for themselves. "Please God, let my child be able to create a life for himself that is fulfilling, that is meaningful, that is—dare I say it—happy."

23

Kyle Mercer:	That's right.
	The most difficult issue that I have to work through with clients, and particularly women, is the judgment on themselves as a bad mother or a good mother.
	It's different for fathers. I'm a man, so my son Henry did not come out of my womb. For women, having that experience of being fully bonded with this person, having them grow inside them, the deepest of bonds, there's this huge pressure around "Good Mother, Bad Mother." As soon as that judgment of Bad Mother comes in, there's guilt associated with it. Then the parenting goes up astronomically. It just keeps on amplifying once we have that judgment of bad mother, because then we want to fix it. That's where this co-dependent parenting comes along. I would say, for you personally, you're stubbornly trying to forgive yourself in some way for something.
Karen Tolchin:	Yes, absolutely. I'm a working mom, which brings its own boatload of guilt. On a deeper level, I brought Charlie into this world and then saddled him with cystic fibrosis. Bad Mother.
	I always get a profound sense of relief in our calls when you press me to embrace the thing I fear most. Whether it's Bad Mother, Bad Daughter, Bad Wife, Bad Employee, whatever horror I'm trying to fend off... I find out very quickly in our conversations that all the energy it's taking to engage with that fear, I get to have all that energy back if I just say, "Okay, I'm bad."
Kyle Mercer:	That's right.

We have children so we can enjoy them, not serve them.

Karen Tolchin: If I just embrace it, it loses all of its power.

Kyle Mercer: You know, on a related note, most of us in our culture at some level are carrying around negative energy stemming from the belief that we're a victim of the parenting we received. That's part of what I do with Inquiry

Method coaching: to free individuals from being a victim of anything that's happened in their past.

Karen Tolchin: I love how Diane first described your coaching to me. She said, "Psychotherapy helps you cope with the obstacles in your life. By contrast, Inquiry Method coaching helps you remove them."

Kyle Mercer: I like that definition.

Karen Tolchin: It's like, why should you just leave your obstacles sitting around in your psyche like outdated furniture, when you could just get rid of them altogether? At first, I was skeptical that it could be done, but I grow less skeptical every week. I'm just feeling lighter and lighter. More powerful.

Kyle Mercer: Great! That's great.

Karen Tolchin: So you're saying, "Get rid of those poisonous ideas." It became much easier for me to drop grievances against my parents the moment I became a parent myself. I think most of us gain a large measure of understanding and acceptance for our parents when we see just how very hard

25

the job is. We're less inclined to see ourselves as victims of any sort of malice, but we still might see ourselves as victims of our parents' limited abilities. You know, their limited skills, their limited knowledge.

Kyle Mercer: Yes, but even that reduced amount of victimhood is still too much. When we really do this work more deeply, eventually we're freed from any resentment, any entanglement, any effect of our childhood. We can be *totally* free from it. We initiate this process with ourselves where we're unconditionally accepting and loving of ourselves. How we were parented becomes a total non-issue the moment that we do that.

Karen Tolchin: But we can still love our parents. I'm a very attachment-oriented sort of person, so freeing myself from those notions initially felt like cutting myself off from the people who loved me.

When business owners tell me they run their companies like a family, I say, "Oh no! Don't do that!"

Kyle Mercer: That's a common reaction.

Karen Tolchin: It was really important for me to understand that this wasn't a rejection of my family. I think that's true both as a child looking at your own parents, and as a parent looking at your own child. You have to understand that the kind of detaching that you're advocating is actually *more* loving. It's a far more loving act than the sort of suffocating, codependent helicopter-mom sort of attachment that our culture seems steeped in at the moment.

Kyle Mercer: That's right. It's important to clarify that I'm not advocating child abandonment. I'm talking about holding things in a different context—a richer, more grounded, more authentic context.

Karen Tolchin: The moment seems ripe for a healthier context for parenting. Could you describe what that might look like?

Kyle Mercer: Yes, but first, I just want to emphasize a point right here that I think is profound. It's this: As we parent our children in a new way, we re-parent ourselves.

Karen Tolchin: That's seems like the heart of the matter right there.

Kyle Mercer: I want to make that really clear, that this doesn't just extend to our children. Literally, to be able to do this—to create a space of deep acceptance for our children, to relate in an organic, authentic way with them—we first must do it with ourselves. Otherwise, we won't be able to use this non-parenting method as a parenting method. We have to own it, and we have to integrate it into the way we live, act, and treat others. It even applies to the workplace. This is universal. These concepts are universal concepts, but the critical path is not to infect our children with false ideas to begin with. The goal is to get the whole culture to shift, and to put me (and others who do similar work) out of business.

Karen Tolchin: What's fascinating to me is that we seem to recreate the family paradigm everywhere in our lives—in school, in work, in religion, in athletics… It's part of our language. You know, "Our Father who art in heaven." We see the whole world in these family terms.

Anybody demanding respect is completely out to lunch.

We look at our bosses very often as the *pater familias*.

Kyle Mercer: That's right. I work with business owners all the time, and they tell me they run their companies like a family. I say, "Oh no! Don't do that!"

Karen Tolchin: We're just duplicating the primary dysfunction, aren't we? We're overly comfortable with this, very often, very hierarchical paradigm. Even in the twenty-first century, it's often a patriarchal structure, with the father and then the mother, and then the eldest son, and then down from there.

Kyle Mercer: We have to be a little careful here. There is truth, and meaning, and value, not in hierarchy-for-hierarchy's sake, but rather in a mentoring relationship. We are supposed to be in a ladder structure interacting with people at a higher spiritual level than we're operating. We can totally honor the people who have gone before us. There can be a deep respect, a deep honoring for those who have accumulated learning. We have very much lost that in our contemporary version of society, where commerce reigns supreme. As we regain this, it's kind of parallel the moment we **stop parenting**, but we start giving people respect.

I so feel that with my son. With Henry, there's a reverent respect he has for me, not because I imposed it on him, but because I'm worthy of it.

Karen Tolchin: Actually, if you tried to impose respect on Henry, it probably wouldn't work. So, it's not necessarily the hierarchy or the ladder, it's the *artificial imposition* of a hierarchy instead of an earned position of honor. You know, the sort of ham-fisted gesture of, "You will listen to me because I am your father."

Kyle Mercer: Anybody demanding respect is completely out to lunch.

Karen Tolchin: This seems really important. You're not saying, "Okay, treat your children as if they are your equals in every way." You're saying, "*Earn* your child's respect as a parent, and start by giving him respect." Be someone your child naturally respects.

Kyle Mercer: Yes, that's right.

The idea is to be very present with our children without controlling them. They want our attention and presence.

Karen Tolchin: Maybe it's because we made them and we diaper them, but it's easy to forget that there is something equally worthy of respect in your child, his or her spiritual essence or soul. He's equally worthy of respect just because he's a human being.

Kyle Mercer: Let's not constantly manipulate and control our children. Instead of being a person to resist, let's be a person to emulate. They see how it is naturally: that we're more effective at operating in the world. They say, "I want some of that." If you wait for your child to ask you a question,

and then answer it, they will appreciate it, and they will ask you for more. If you start trying to manipulate and control your child, you're going to be rejected and they're going to push away all the things that you could potentially have to offer. Not only are you squandering the opportunity to have this wonderful mentoring interaction with your child, but you're also having them rebelliously push you away.

Karen Tolchin: That really gets to the heart of the matter. That happens so often because we think, "Oh, if I'm going to be a decent parent, I need to teach my child this and that..."

Kyle Mercer: I want to make something really clear, here. The purity of this starts with an infant, or even in the womb. These issues do not appear in any way that creates struggle unless we haven't proceeded in this way.

If we're starting out with a high school student, applying this approach, it's a remediation. You can't just start at this secondary point and have it work beautifully. You have to understand that this is a cultural, mental shift, and it's challenging in the same way that it is for us to do our own work to develop and grow. As soon as we set the context for our teenager to grow and evolve, that's a challenge. They're going to have to go back through a bunch of pain, and hurt, and unlearn a bunch of things, because they've already been accumulating things.

In essence, the earlier the better.

Karen Tolchin: Ideally, this book would go out to all newly expectant parents instead of *What To Expect When You're Expecting*.

CONVERSATION #3

From the Abstract to
the Concrete,
or, When Henry Bit Matthew[2]

One of the best things about talking with Kyle—as opposed to lying
on a couch delivering a monologue to a silent Freudian analyst—
is that he frequently shares stories from his own life to illustrate a difficult concept. He's fearless about revealing his own personal struggles,
and his stories show that he's always learning and growing, too. They
also show him in action as a very unusual sort of parent.

One aspect of Kyle's theories that I'm really struggling with putting
into practice in my own life is the whole "let the world teach your child"
and "let your child find his inner truth" business. I recognize the value
in both, but I'm finding it hard to trust both the world and my son.
When I first became a parent, I was shocked to see how cruel children
can be to each other. Clearly, I repressed this knowledge from my own
childhood as soon as I became an adult.

I am the mother of a rough and tumble boy. Because I've tried
to exert so much control over his health, he's tried to grab what little
power he can, and he's become resistant and oppositional. He's smart
and sweet and funny and loving, but he's also challenging me on a
daily basis. Just getting him to put on his socks in the morning can
wear me out for the better part of the day. Worst of all, he's decided
to root for the bad guys in every story possibly because he sees how

---

[2]   Not his real name.

much this disturbs me. I'm a pacifist, but I'm raising a boy who roots for Hook, not Pan.

What keeps me up at night is this thought: "What if the world fails to teach my child the right lessons? What if Charlie's truth turns out to be that he never wants to share his toys, or that maybe he likes hitting other people, or worse? Shouldn't I be actively shaping him to curb those impulses?" Clearly, I've been programmed to be the sort of mom who says, "Share even if you don't feel like sharing." Should I let myself be deprogrammed, or will I just end up condemning Charlie to misery on Death Row, all because I never taught him that being an ax murderer is wrong?

Karen Tolchin: So, I'm having trouble trusting that the world will teach Charlie what he needs to know, and that he will make the right choices when it comes to interacting with others. My impulse as a teacher is so clearly to shape, and to make sure that he shares his toys, doesn't hurt people, etc.

Kyle Mercer: There's a different approach you can take. At the forefront is the principle that it's less ideal for the parent to be setting that boundary.

Karen Tolchin: So, I should be letting the world teach my child that hoarding his toys is wrong, that biting is wrong, etc.?

Kyle Mercer: Well, you could let the world show him that it's ineffective.

Let the world socialize the child.

At a young age, my son Henry went through a biting stage. There is a developmental stage where the only potent thing you can do is bite. You're not strong enough to hit or shove. The only thing that can get anybody else's attention is a bite. A lot of kids go through a biting stage because they discover it's powerful.

We were over at a friend's house, and Henry bit another child, and the parent was just outraged. But what I knew is that the other child, Matthew, was always doing things to test boundaries and to get at Henry. Finally, Henry just got tired of it and hauled off and bit Matthew. He was setting a boundary, having been ignored when he tried to set it in other ways. When Henry bit him, Matthew got direct feedback that his actions weren't working.

Karen Tolchin: There's nothing ambiguous about a bite.

Kyle Mercer: Matthew's mom wanted to take away Henry's ability to take care of himself away by outlawing biting. This often happens when a child bites: there's this fear that he's a biter now, and he's going to turn into a mass murderer when he grows up. Well, this isn't what creates mass murderers.

Karen Tolchin: Okay, as a neurotic mom, I have to stop you there and ask: What *does* create a mass murderer?

Kyle Mercer: Well, let's say there is a child that, because of his circumstances, is full of rage and anger. Well, we need to deal with that rage and anger.

34

Karen Tolchin: So, what you're saying is, if your kid is simply going through a normal phase and happens to haul off and bite somebody, don't hit the panic button and speak or act from a place of fear.

Kyle Mercer: Exactly. Now, if your child is running around hitting people and hurting people all the time, yeah, we need to set a boundary with him, but the boundary isn't predicated on the belief that the child is inherently bad. You set the boundary around yourself: "It's not working for me for you to hit other people."

Karen Tolchin: It's subtle, but it seems like an important shift.

Kyle Mercer: That's right. We don't say, "You're a bad boy for hitting." The energy should be on, "This hitting behavior is not working."

Setting boundaries for other people is control. Setting boundaries for yourself is self care.

Karen Tolchin: I see, like, "It's making it hard for us to get through our day." Totally different from, "Oh God, what if the truth about you is that you're innately bad and will become an ax murderer?"

Kyle Mercer: That's right: draw the boundary around yourself.

Karen Tolchin: So basically, Matthew's mom wanted to shame Henry for protecting himself. I mean, Henry wasn't doing it in a very socially acceptable way, but he *was* trying to establish that boundary. So, I'm curious. What did you say to Matthew's mom?

Kyle Mercer: I didn't say much. I just felt as if that was okay feedback for Henry to receive, but I didn't feel any need to correct Henry about it.

Karen Tolchin: I'm amazed that you were able to stay so calm in that scenario. I would have fallen all over myself apologizing. Then, I would have launched into a disquisition on why we are pacifists in our family and don't bite.

Henry saw for himself that when you bite other children, it causes a ruckus. Their parents go ballistic. It's that direct experience with the world you're talking about. As his dad, you didn't feel the need to pile on and go ballistic yourself.

Kyle Mercer: That's right. Henry's just learning that if he bites people, sometimes other people get upset. That's fine. He's not getting the message that there is something wrong with him. It's not coming from the parental love zone that he's broken. Do you see the difference?

Karen Tolchin: I do.

Kyle Mercer: Here's another biting story for you.

One time we were in a hotel and I used the electronic key card, and Henry always liked doing that, and he got upset with me for not letting him have the fun of using the key card. He was in his biting phase, and he came right at me at crotch level, full speed, with his mouth open. I was going to get bitten in the crotch!

Karen Tolchin: Oh, no! Not good.

It's no wonder we're such unempowered, uninspired, unalive human beings, considering the conflicting messages we receive as children.

Kyle Mercer: Not good. So, I put out my arm, I straight-armed him, and he fell back onto his butt. I said, "I don't want to be bitten." He never tried to bite me again.

Karen Tolchin: So, the difference is between saying, "I don't want to be bitten,"—between drawing the boundary around yourself—versus saying, "Don't be a bad boy, biting is bad…"

Kyle Mercer: Or else, "Never bite." That's not true! We don't want to tell our children never to bite. Sometimes it's *important* to bite, to protect yourself.

Karen Tolchin: Absolutely. This is an extreme example, but I was a rape crisis counselor in college, and we had some self-defense training. We were told that as women, we've been conditioned to be ladylike and pleasing, even when we're being attacked. One of the best things we can actually do is to be as *unladylike* as possible—to bite, vomit, urinate, whatever it takes.

Kyle Mercer: That's more of that unlearning we were talking about. Unlearn that you have to be nice even when someone is being violent towards you.

Karen Tolchin:	Exactly. Maybe the shaping that we do as parents actually takes away our children's power. It can make them more vulnerable in a world that can be dangerous.
Kyle Mercer:	There are infinite smaller examples. At the Mountain Experience, we create a list as a group of all the ideas that contradict themselves. "Speak up, say what you mean, but don't talk so loud. Tell the truth, but don't tell Grandma that she smells bad. Tell the truth, but don't express anger with your parents." There are layers upon layers of these thoughts and ideas that just jam us up and lock up our systems.
	It's no wonder we're such unempowered, uninspired, unalive human beings.
Karen Tolchin:	No wonder we're so agitated.
Kyle Mercer:	Well, it makes us neurotic. If you think about it, if I am in an interaction with somebody and I've got thirty ideas that are incompatible and they're running around in my head, how can I ever put together any kind of sentence or communication that has any value?
Karen Tolchin:	So, a lot of the parenting that we do is actually creating huge confusion in our kids. We tell them one thing, and they know on some level that it's not true for them, but if they want our love and our acceptance, they've got to somehow make themselves fit.
Kyle Mercer:	That's it. I love what Alan Watts said about this. Parents tell this huge, huge lie. The lie is, "I want you to be yourself and be happy to conform." Impossible, it's just impossible. You can't be

	yourself and also be happy to conform. Actually what we want as a culture is to have you *not* be an individual; we want you to be like everybody else.
Karen Tolchin:	I'm beginning to see how the way we parent just sends message after message to our children that they are not okay. No wonder we are all so conflicted.
Kyle Mercer:	It's all conditional love.
Karen Tolchin:	It's conditional love, and the conditions are impossible to meet. It's like, "Good luck with *that*!"
Kyle Mercer:	Exactly.
Karen Tolchin:	We're all being set up for failure.

Tantrum in Aisle Nine

The beauty and simplicity of Kyle's philosophy evaporates for me when my son pitches an epic fit out in public. I've been raised to believe that only the worst parent sits idly by while her child throws a public tantrum, and I'm in a constant state of anxiety about what to do. During their visits, my parents have begun to suggest that a good spanking would do wonders for their grandson.

"We don't do that in my generation of parents," I say. "We have time-outs, we revoke privileges, we have other things…"

"How's that working for you?" they ask. The truth is, not well at all, but I'm still not going to raise my hand against my child. Tom is less sure about this stance, and it's causing extra stress in our marriage.

The prevailing parenting wisdom is that it will cripple your child for life if you don't teach him good boundaries. It will also advertise to the world that you are a failure as a parent, a failure as a human being. In other words, "parent" is an active verb, and if you're too passive, you'll fail your children. Even though very few voices are still advocating spanking, there's still a strong flavor of, "Spare the rod, spoil the child."

Kyle is saying something radically different from my parenting sources in a lot of respects, first among them being that your job as a parent is to be shaping your children at every turn. That seems like the essence of modern parenting: to get in there even when it's uncomfortable. Even when it makes you the bad guy. "Don't be a friend, be a parent"—that's a major theme, illustrated by such real-life cautionary *tales as Lindsay Lohan and other high-profile children whose parents joined the party instead of actively parenting.*

In this conversation, I ask for help. I press Kyle to give me a concrete example of how to handle a typical parental crisis: the dreaded Grocery Store Meltdown. When we first embarked on this book project, I was completely obsessed with having this particular problem solved. It's funny to reread this transcript and see how difficult it was to get Kyle to answer the question. It's equally funny to see how stubbornly I refuse to drop the subject. It's as if I believe that the answer to this one question will magically transform all of my parenting quandaries.

In a way, it does.

Karen Tolchin: Could you walk us through a **Stop Parenting** approach to the grocery store meltdown scenario? Think of the two-year-old who is used to having all of his needs met, because he's basically been a blob of ectoplasm up to this point. He wakes up, he gets a new diaper when he's wet, he gets food when he's hungry… That's how the world has existed for him in a lot of ways. Coming in contact with the outside world, being bombarded as we all are with advertisements and enticements to consume, that's when the first primal conflict arises for many of us. All of a sudden, the harmony breaks between parent and child.

With your approach, how much skill does your child need to have? How much reason, how much understanding?

Kyle Mercer: Zero! Zero reasoning and understanding is appropriate.

Karen Tolchin: Great! Except now you have to explain that to me, because I'm totally lost.

41

Kyle Mercer: Okay. So we think that we need to teach our children reason and understanding, and that's the biggest problem. They need no reason and understanding. It is not a mental process. This is an organic process that affects our way of being. We get it physically, emotionally, mentally, spiritually, on all these levels, and I see people talking to their two-year-olds as if they're college students. I'm not saying it's the talking that's the problem, but a two-year-old has no concept of tomorrow. "If you do this today, this will happen tomorrow." Absolutely not within their realm. It's total insanity. It's like having a conversation with your dog about why it peed on the floor. It's irrelevant.

Karen Tolchin: I can understand that.

Kyle Mercer: Remember the Charlie Brown specials? All you hear from the teacher is "Wha, wha, wha, wha, wha, wha."

Karen Tolchin: Okay, so I'm your child. We're in Walmart together and I see something shiny.

Kyle Mercer: I'm going to be difficult here, but, part of my principle is, I don't have anything in my world for my child to relate to that I don't want to have. Walmart is a terrible place for a child to be. Like a background principle, let's just start with food for a second, is, why have anything at my house that I don't want anybody eating?

Karen Tolchin: Right. Don't have Twinkies in the pantry if you want your kid to eat real food. I think what you're describing is living with more integrity, thinking about our choices, being more mindful and more present…

Kyle Mercer:	That's right. I'm going to give a different example if I can. I was out to dinner with my two-year-old. There's this formal dinner, we're all dressed up, we're sitting around the table at a fancy restaurant, and he was restless. Well, of course! He was two years old, for God's sake.
Karen Tolchin:	Right. That's when you can only legitimately ask them to sit still for approximately two minutes.

Children run the unspoken energy in the home.

Kyle Mercer:	Why would you ask them to sit still at all? It makes absolutely no sense. Again, just insanity. They have no concept of sitting still, their ability to sit still is probably twenty seconds, and their mind's going to be off to the next thing. Then you're going to get angry at them, and they're not going to understand why you're angry at them. Then, now they're running the angry energy—
Karen Tolchin:	I love that, "Running the angry energy." You've told me before that children run the unspoken energy in a household, so you can actually look at a child acting out and see what isn't getting talked about in a family. I see that now all the time.
Kyle Mercer:	That's right. So you're at dinner, and now you're just stuck with anger. Pretty quickly, you're on this terrible loop. So if you want to go out to dinner with a two or three-year-old, you sit down, you

order, you give them some crayons when they feel like sitting still, and when they want to start making noise, you take them outside and go throw breadcrumbs for the ducks until the food arrives. Then hopefully dinner will be interesting enough to hold their attention.

The problem is that we're trying to form the kids and get them to be like we want them to be. You have to accept the kid.

Karen Tolchin: So this is what you're getting at when you say, "Cultivate a deep acceptance of your child." Don't try to get him to show up for you in the way you think you need him to show up. He is not a short adult.

Kyle Mercer: Exactly. Nor is *my* two-year-old like *your* two-year-old.

Karen Tolchin: That's so true, especially if I have a boy and you have a girl. I'm forever amazed by little girls' capacity for sitting quietly at restaurants. They're sitting with bows in their hair, coloring like little angels, while my son and all the other boys are doing laps around the restaurant, toppling trays, etc. It's almost funny. Almost.

Kyle Mercer: There are only a few small children who would contentedly sit through dinner looking with rapt amazement at all the adults, just soaking it all up. Well, that's great if you have that particular kind of child. If you've got one that wants to run around at full speed all the time then you'd better skip the formal dinners and only take him places where he can run around at full speed.

Every child looks for a way to get a hook into his or her parent. Get unhookable.

Karen Tolchin: I agree with that 100%, and I would either skip the fancy dinner or get a sitter if I could. But—and I don't mean to be a broken record here—there are times when ordinary parents have to take their kids into a grocery store. So my question is, what would be an appropriate, **Stop Parenting** response to the kid throwing a tantrum in Aisle Nine?

Kyle Mercer: My son, at three, had a little phase. This is another thing to understand: Kids go through phases, and if you as an individual, can't go grow through their phase with them, they're stuck with their phase. When a child is going through a phase, it's not about changing him. It's going to take patience, and you have to grow to be big enough so that he doesn't run that energy anymore.

Another basic truth about kids is this: Children are programmed to find the chink in the adult's armor so that they can get control, so that they can manage and control their world, so that they won't be abandoned. They're testing the attention. Each child fundamentally is always looking for a way to get the hook into his or her parent. So, if you, as a parent, react to something, if your child gets your goat, he'll go, "Ah-ha! I've got to try this again!" If it works better and better,

45

they're going to stay with it until *you* have grown through it.

Parenting is the sweetest process of personal growth. It's not about the child growing. It's really that *they're* forcing *you* to grow up and be more magnanimous or bigger, more accepting, more loving, more patient, more spacious, more spiritual.

Karen Tolchin: And more adaptable. Surviving phase after phase really requires you to adapt. That's one of my own trouble spots.

Kyle Mercer: I want to be very precise about the language in this book, and "adaptable" doesn't have the right nuance. Adaptable means, "I'm being modified by the child in some way." It's *not* about us adapting to our child. It's about us growing into a big enough space where we have the capacity to hold the context for what's happening.

Karen Tolchin: I'm confused. How is what you just said different from being adaptable?

Kyle Mercer: Adaptable, to me, implies that I'm being flexible and becoming modified by the environment. I'm talking about growing to a higher stage where I see it from a higher perspective and am able to hold a wiser, larger, broader, expanded view.

Parenting is the sweetest process of personal growth. It's not about the children growing: it's that they're forcing you to grow up.

It's just like the child. If you're walking along and there's a three-foot railing and they can't see the dog coming up from the other side, you pick them up and say, "There's a dog coming. I've got you." They think that you're some kind of omniscient god, right?

Karen Tolchin: It's kind of great.

Kyle Mercer: It's just because you're three feet taller than they are, right? This would be the same thing. You have to grow so that you have the altitude to have the wisdom to move gracefully and harmoniously through that situation. I'll give you another example, we'll go back to the grocery store.

Karen Tolchin: Hooray! The grocery store.

Kyle Mercer: At three years old, Henry was going through what I call the "Protest Moment" phase. At some point he got a little traction with either his mom or me. If he made a big fuss, we didn't know what to do, and we tried to fix it. We were in Safeway, and I don't even remember what the issue was, maybe it was a shiny object or something, and I just said, "Oh, we're not getting that." Henry got down on the floor, and started pounding on it,

47

saying, "Arggh!!!" Everybody's looking at this child. Now, if my ego's attached that I'm the kind of parent who would raise a child who would get down on the floor and scream and yell, I'm going to try and get him to shut up or give him the shiny object so nobody knows I'm a bad parent. Fortunately, I had already accepted that I'm a bad parent. I just stood there, going, "Oh, you're having a protest moment!" It was helpful to name it. I said, "I'm sorry, Sweetie. I'll wait." I just waited until he was done. I walked around and checked my emails.

Karen Tolchin: This will be the first parenting book in history ever written by a self-proclaimed bad parent. Two for the price of one, actually. Where does the power come from, in that phrase? It feels very powerful, "I had already accepted that I'm a bad parent."

Kyle Mercer: It's an irony, really, for this reason: The idea of good or bad parents, even parents in our modern way, it's just a stand-in for an egoic identity. It doesn't mean anything. I'm not a good parent or a bad parent; I'm just Kyle. I'm just a being who has a child named Henry. As long as you've got an idea of what parents should be like, or what they should do, you lose flexibility and creativity.

Your children need your acceptance. Then you can either be happy or unhappy about what they're like.

If I'm holding onto that identity, that I'm some-one who shapes and forms the other being into a decent human being... But I'm rejecting that. As a parent, you can say—beyond bad or good—I'm a very accepting parent.

Karen Tolchin: I'm sure Henry appreciates that quality in you.

Kyle Mercer: Maybe I'm not always even that. Sometimes I can't accept. But that would be the ideal: the accepting parent. As soon as I think I'm sup-posed to be a good or bad parent, not only do I judge myself, but I also judge my child. This is the hardest one. I can't tell you how many times I've infuriated people because I said, "You need to accept that you're a bad parent." They simply won't even talk to me anymore.

Karen Tolchin: I can understand that. It's so hard to process, the temptation is to reject it outright.

Kyle Mercer: What I'm really saying is, "You're no parent at all, you're just a human being!" You're a human being that loves and accepts this other little human being that you produced, and you're just being a human being. It's your job to grow up enough to provide a context for this person.

    You're going to love this. This weekend, I told this whole group of business people to grow up and be happy.

Karen Tolchin: Wow! How'd they take it?

Kyle Mercer: Pretty well, actually.

    Here's what it really means to grow up. You have three choices in life: You either change it, you accept it, or you be unhappy. Your children need to be accepted, and then you can either be

	happy about what they're like or not be happy about it.
Karen Tolchin:	It doesn't get much clearer than that.
Kyle Mercer:	There's one, maybe just one factor in being the "Good parent," and that is being happy.
Karen Tolchin:	Happy in what they've got with their kids? Happy in general?
Kyle Mercer:	Actually, happy is an interesting word. The more fundamental aspect is total acceptance of what's true. Content with what is. A radical openness to what's true is even better than acceptance.
Karen Tolchin:	So if you only have these three choices in all areas of life, to change, to accept/be open, or to be unhappy… When you apply that to parenting, it's not actually three choices, right? If I understand you, you can't change a person.
Kyle Mercer:	No, you can't ever change people. Only they can decide if they want to change. But you can change some circumstances. For instance, if your child likes to run around the house, and you have a china collection on the coffee table, you can either be really unhappy, or you can change it and just put the china away until they're eighteen.
Karen Tolchin:	In other words, street smarts. Just not in the streets, but in your living room.
Kyle Mercer:	Street smarts in your living room.

CONVERSATION #5

Your Kid's Education is
His Own #%$! Business

Kyle's take on education is a total reversal of the helicopter-parent norm. It always seemed to me that the most basic service parents can perform for their kids is to shepherd them through a successful K-12 education. Getting the kid up in the morning, fed, dressed, and to class on time and prepared with finished homework and gym shoes, etc. How could we stop doing all of that and not harm a child for life? When I was a child, I'm sure I would have chosen to stay home, eat junk food, and watch General Hospital. Wouldn't I?

At the same time, it's becoming more and more clear that everything I believe I'm doing in my child's best interests is actually more about my own interests. This is a sobering realization, to say the least.

Kyle uses everything but a crowbar to get me to separate from my son just enough to see that my own happiness/education should be my main focus, not his. As far as his education is concerned, my job is not to interfere. In this conversation, our topics range far and wide, from homeschooling to ADHD.

Karen Tolchin: I came into parenting thinking one of my jobs would be to help Charlie with his homework, to make sure that he did it on time, etc. We were all told that if you do your homework and you get into Harvard, and you obtain the Harvard degree, then you'll be a happy person.

Kyle Mercer: That's one of those faulty beliefs that we were talking about. Does everybody who has a

Harvard degree end up happy? No, absolutely not.

Karen Tolchin: I remember you once telling me that you've worked with a lot of miserable Harvard grads, or equally accomplished people who are unhappy. They were externally compelled to be driven as students, by Tiger Mom-ish parents, and then they woke up as adults saying, "How the heck did I get here? I don't want to be a concert pianist!" They don't have an intrinsic desire to be doing what their whole lives were set up for them to be doing.

Kyle Mercer: That's right. They're just buried under a mountain of these ideas that have been foisted on them, instead of listening to what's true for them.

Karen Tolchin: You've spoken really meaningfully about how you put Henry and Henry's teachers in charge of his education. First, you and Henry's mom chose a Waldorf school for him, which prizes the child's whole development as an individual. Then, you made it clear that you wouldn't interfere with his teachers—questioning his grades, etc.

Kyle Mercer: That's right. I would tell his teacher at the start of every new school year, "This is between you and Henry."

Karen Tolchin: I can see the value in not being a helicopter mom, but just taking myself out of the equation completely? You've also told me that you would never say to him, "Hey, do your homework."

Kyle Mercer: Right. It has nothing to do with me.

Karen Tolchin: "It has nothing to do with me. Henry does his homework if he wants to do his homework."

	You've just effectively walked away from a huge battleground for parents.
Kyle Mercer:	Yes, I have. Now, sometimes if I saw him being frustrated, I would say, "I see you are frustrated or upset. What's going on?" He might say, "Well, I haven't gotten my homework done." I would say, "Well, do you want to do it?" Then, Henry could come up with why he wanted to do his homework, or not.
Karen Tolchin:	We're living in a cultural moment where it's totally normal for parents to do the homework alongside their children every night. Parents are actually complaining to teachers about the workload because they're the ones doing so much of it, after a full day of adult work.
Kyle Mercer:	That's just wrong.
	At the same time, there's a wave and a movement of children and young people coming up that are much less indoctrinated than we were. It's really interesting. I know recently they've done polls and young people coming out of college nowadays are much more interested in the meaning of what they're going to be doing than the pay for what they're going to be doing.
	It shows the huge cultural shift that's occurring. I do believe that things are changing in the same way our generation, how we were parented, was a big improvement on how our parents were parented.
Karen Tolchin:	It does seem there is *some* progress...

| Kyle Mercer: | There *is* progress. It's not all dismal and hopeless. I think it's part of the reason why people will read this book. People are looking for a better way. |

Everyone is responsible for his or her own well-being.

Karen Tolchin:	Jennifer Senior points out that, not long ago in human history, people had kids to work their farms. By contrast, nowadays children are (in a phrase she quotes often) "economically useless but emotionally priceless." So, now the whole family is oriented around the happiness of the child. She talks about how the parents used to be like the employers and the kids were the employees. Now, it's almost as if the children are the employers and the parents are racing around like the employees.
Kyle Mercer:	This is where we're getting all of these narcissistic children who totally believe that they're entitled to be served. That's exactly it.
Karen Tolchin:	It's an epidemic of narcissism and entitlement. I think the helicopter mom is actually more like the Marine One pilot employed by her child, the President. She's in perpetual service, hovering nearby, trying to be useful for the child. So, even though I do think we are getting better generation after generation, we're not quite there yet.
Kyle Mercer:	They're little kings and queens, and they become little tyrants. It's just a matter of letting them have

	their own experience so that we can get on with our lives. Yeah, we've got kids, we're going to make sure they're fed. Make sure they don't run in front of a train.
Karen Tolchin:	Right.
Kyle Mercer:	Then enjoy our lives. But we make our whole lives about them. It's the same. Think about somebody that makes their whole life about their dog, right? What is that like?
Karen Tolchin:	Special dog outfits, and dog accessories.
Kyle Mercer:	We have children so we can enjoy them, not serve them.
Karen Tolchin:	I just realized hearing you say all that, that this whole project for me has still been about how can I do this better, how can I get this right, so *Charlie* does better, so *Charlie* is happier. It really has not occurred to me until you articulated it that plainly that what we're really talking about is, how can I make my *own* life better?
Kyle Mercer:	Exactly. If we come back to the whole narcissistic thing, why do you want Charlie to be happy?
Karen Tolchin:	I don't know, I just do. I guess it would say good things about me.
Kyle Mercer:	Well, then, if it says good things about you, you think that's going to make you what?
Karen Tolchin:	Happy. Good mother, happy mother.
Kyle Mercer:	Again, it's all about making you happy, but it's just so indirect.
Karen Tolchin:	It's all about me, no matter what, I acknowledge that. There's no real altruism in parenting.

Kyle Mercer:	It is, it's all about you being happy. Let's cut out the middle man.
Karen Tolchin:	I've got to clean up whatever thoughts I have that I'm not doing this for myself.
Kyle Mercer:	Right.
Kyle Mercer:	There's another possible title for this book: "Parenting for Happiness." Or, "Stop Parenting, Be Happy." As soon as you make your happiness contingent on Charlie's happiness, what's the chance of being happy?
Karen Tolchin:	Zero.
Kyle Mercer:	You're out of luck if that's your approach.
Karen Tolchin:	That's pretty sobering...
	But you know, I'm still seeing bad mothers represented on television and in film, as cautionary tales, and reflexively thinking, "I wouldn't want to be anything like that." Last week, there was a mother on the television show *Nashville* who was all about herself, very narcissistic, and did not make sure that her child had what she needed in a very basic way. She was an alcoholic, so in many ways she was just incapable.
	My reaction was still pretty profound, like, "Ohhh, that person was selfish and her child suffered. That's what *not* to be." How do you strike the right balance?
Kyle Mercer:	There's no balance.
Karen Tolchin:	There's *no* balance?
Kyle Mercer:	There's zero balance. It's all about your happiness.
Karen Tolchin:	I have a hard time accepting that—

Kyle Mercer:	I'm sure you do!
Karen Tolchin:	—because of the love I feel for Charlie. I don't want it to be all about me, I want it to be all about Charlie, on some deep level.
Kyle Mercer:	It's still all about you.
Karen Tolchin:	Maybe I believe Charlie deserves it more than I do. Charlie deserves my attention more than I do.
Kyle Mercer:	So that's how badly you feel about yourself. And why does he deserve it?
Karen Tolchin:	Because he's this fresh, new person on the planet.
Kyle Mercer:	Why does he deserve it?
Karen Tolchin:	Because he was born deserving it. No reason. He was just born deserving it. Which I suppose I was as well…
Kyle Mercer:	"He was born deserving it, but I wasn't."
Karen Tolchin:	In some crazy way, that must be what I believe.
Kyle Mercer:	You are flawed, there's something wrong with you, but there's nothing wrong with him. It's just a silly idea that one person can be born deserving something more than another. In fact, it's not about deserving it, even. It's just like, if you come upon a mango plantation, there's mangoes everywhere that you're invited to take. You go, "I don't deserve a mango, or else I do deserve it." I deserve to be here because I've worked very hard.

It's neither! You don't *deserve* it or *not deserve* it, it just *is*. Deserving is a fallacy. |

57

Karen Tolchin:	I think what I'm concerned about is that if I actually do this, if I parent for happiness, for myself, then Charlie is not going to get something that he really needs.
Kyle Mercer:	Then what will happen?
Karen Tolchin:	Well, disaster.
Kyle Mercer:	What kind of disaster?
Karen Tolchin:	He will grow up to be miserable and unhappy and ...
Kyle Mercer:	Let's look at children who get everything. Beyond what they need, everything that they want. What happens?
Karen Tolchin:	That's a different kind of disaster. We worry about that, raising our child in a very affluent town. He's bound to come to us at some point and say, "Where's my Maserati?"
Kyle Mercer:	People didn't used to have a lot of possessions or get attached to things, or all this kind of stuff. It's a very modern idea. We pay a high price for having all this stuff.

You have to decide between what Charlie needs and what he wants. What kind of things might he need? |
Karen Tolchin:	Shelter, clothing, food, medication.
Kyle Mercer:	Okay, so what's the chance of him not getting those things?
Karen Tolchin:	Zero.
Kyle Mercer:	It has nothing to do with what we're talking about. It has nothing to do with fawning, and doting, and buying everything he possibly wants. I mean, all these things, in fact, can often

do more damage by, again, creating that narcissistic situation.

At the same time, there is already a movement of people that are parenting less.

Karen Tolchin: That's true. There's a great blog called "Free Range Kids" about not smothering our children, and we hear about the more relaxed French way of parenting described in *Bringing up Bébé*... There are also schools like your son Henry's Waldorf school that seem to be oriented around giving children more of a hands-on, direct experience of the world.

Kyle Mercer: It's true, it has a lot of things going for it. Yet you can still see these old beliefs even within the context of the Henry's school. You still see individual teachers that have the same "Fix the Child" mindset.

Karen Tolchin: I'm sure. One of the things I appreciate about Charlie's school is that they really do encourage individual exploration, independent study, designing your own curriculum on robotics if that interests you, all of that. It seems much more respectful than the more traditional pedagogy, the "We know exactly what's right for you, and we're going to force-feed it to you" school.

Kyle Mercer: That sounds good.

Karen Tolchin: So, one place I'm still confused is about the educational role of the parent. How do we give kids the fundamental sense of safe place and deep acceptance that we're supposed to give them while also serving as their parents?

Kyle Mercer:	I don't understand the conflict so you're going to have to clarify that to me.
Karen Tolchin:	This is huge. I think that's the piece I'm still hanging on to. There's still a large component of me that believes I'm here to guide Charlie. That I'm his first teacher, basically, and that I'm here to teach and offer guidance.
Kyle Mercer:	Can I do a little Inquiry with you around that? That may be helpful for the whole thing.
Karen Tolchin:	Of course.
Kyle Mercer:	What is the outcome that you want to guide in your son? What do you want to guide him to?
Karen Tolchin:	To a sense of safety and happiness. To a wonderful place in this world.
Kyle Mercer:	Yes, which is what you want for yourself, right?
Karen Tolchin:	Absolutely. Maybe we can get a two-for-one.
Kyle Mercer:	The way to get him there is to do it yourself and forget all about him. He's going to turn out to be just like you. This comes back to the premise of our book. This is not about learning how to parent your child, this is about getting your act together so you're a decent model.
Karen Tolchin:	So I can lead by example.
Kyle Mercer:	It's not even leading by example, it's just being it. If you be it without foisting it on anybody, it's going to be obviously the natural best way to

If parenting worked, we'd all be enlightened.

live, so other people are going to want to do it. Until you start controlling and creating resistance, they'd be like this. Especially when you're being totally hypocritical and not doing it yourself. Just be it. All the things you said you wanted for your child are things you haven't managed to create for yourself, so what makes you think you could teach him?

Karen Tolchin: Right. Right. Yet, I want it so much for him.

Kyle Mercer: Actually, you want it so much for *you*. That's the truth.

Karen Tolchin: I want it so much for both of us.

Kyle Mercer: You want it for you. It's why you get so attached, and why you're giving yourself away to him. "I don't have it, but maybe I can make it happen in him and it will be kind of like I had it." It's a huge hypocrisy that all these parents are trying to drum into their children. It's all the things they aren't. You can't teach something until you've been it. If you're totally blissed out and happy and grounded in life and at peace and untriggerable and zenned out, and have great friends and clean relationships, your kids will, too. They have to go through their own experiences to have it. How much of your parent's advice did you take?

Karen Tolchin: I'm not sure. Not that much, probably.

Kyle Mercer: You had to figure it out for yourself. If parenting worked, we'd all be enlightened. Our parents told us all the things we should do and said, "If you do these things then you'll be happy," and it didn't work. If parenting worked, I'd be 100% behind it.

Karen Tolchin:	Sure. I know you just explicitly told me to stop teaching my child, but the next parenting question I have written down for you hinges on the verb "teach."
Kyle Mercer:	Lay it on me.
Karen Tolchin:	How do we teach kids awareness of their inner source of knowing?
Kyle Mercer:	We don't. They are inherently aware.
Karen Tolchin:	They know it already? That's another thing I found remarkable at the Mountain Experience, how we've all grown so disconnected from our inner knowing, from our source, and so deeply ashamed of all of our feelings.
Kyle Mercer:	Not grown so. We've been taught to be. By our parenting.
Karen Tolchin:	Right. Children know it already.
Kyle Mercer:	In a way. Inquiry Method is the best way to relate to anybody, including your child. Being curious and interested in what they are. If your child comes to you with a problem, just like if a client comes to me with a problem and I have my teacher part of me, I don't always use Inquiry for efficiency, but if we want to teach our children to think, we can't think for them, right?
Karen Tolchin:	Right.
Kyle Mercer:	They say, "I'm having trouble with my grades." You say, "What's the trouble?" They say, "I've got D's in two of my classes." If you freak out and say, "You've got to get your act together and go study," they never learn anything about how to think. If you want your child to think you say,

"What's the problem with that?" That's the last thing any parent I know would say to a kid coming home with D's.

Karen Tolchin: That's true. I would freak out.

Kyle Mercer: We do not teach our children to think for themselves so they never own why they're getting an A, it's just because you told them to. Maybe they say, "I don't want a D because nobody likes people who get D's." You say, "Why not?" They say, "It makes them stupid." You say, "Are you stupid?" "Yeah, I think I'm stupid." "What's stupid about you?" "It's stupid because I don't know how to do this math." "Really? Have you ever been able to learn things you didn't know how to do before?" "Sure, I learned how to play the guitar." "But you can't learn math?" "I just don't want to." "Okay, great." They say, "But I don't want to get a D." I say, "Do you prefer to get a D or do you prefer to learn math?" They go, "I don't know, let me think about that." Then we come back to why do you want to get good grades again. "I want to be a doctor." "Do doctors need math?" "I'm not sure if they need math." "Why would a doctor learn math?" "So they can get into medical school." "Do you want to get into medical school?" "I'm not sure." "Okay, great."

They can work the whole thing out for themselves. If you just ask them questions, then they come to an awareness of why they're doing things.

When Henry finished middle school, he was heading to high school, and I said, "You don't have to go. I'll hire you private teachers. I want

63

you to do something because I don't want some-body bumming around the house,

but you can do anything you want." Finally he decided to go to high school. He's going to high school because he wanted to. When he has trouble with his grades I say, "What do you want to do about it?" He says, "Maybe I want to quit." I say, "Okay, great. What are you going to do next?" He says, "I don't want to quit because I want to go to college." "Okay. What kind of col-lege?" "I want to go to a good college and I want to get a scholarship."

He cares about things like scholarships because I haven't promised to pay for his schooling. I've said, "You're on your own." He's aware of that. He's even planning for colleges that are econom-ical. I may end up helping him, and he knows I've set aside $15,000 for him, but that's his $15,000 to do what he wants. He owns it all.

Karen Tolchin: What is most striking to me about your part in that dialogue with Henry is the total absence of judgment. How did you get to a place where you are able to be so free of judgment?

Kyle Mercer: Discipline. I'm not always free of it because I still have judgments on myself. I have a judgment on myself that I work harder at life. Since I have that judgment on myself, sometimes that judgment comes up on Henry. It's my judgment on myself. It has nothing to do with him. I've got to work through that.

Karen Tolchin: Do you think that your commitment to keeping yourself clean is like a gift you're giving your son?

Kyle Mercer: Yes. That, and I even try to do more. I make the effort to be, as far as I interact, cleaner than how I feel. I don't project my stuff onto him. I own it as my own dysfunction when I'm not able to use Inquiry, to be an Inquiry parent. That just tells me I have more to grow on. Just like we're talking about. This whole process is about me growing. The more I live my life in my bliss, the more authentic my relationship with Henry is, the more it serves all of us.

Karen Tolchin: It seems as if the best thing we can do is to shift the focus from our child to ourselves. That would suggest that something like home schooling might be a step in the wrong direction, because it's so child-centered. What's your take on home schooling?

We have an educational system that serves 10% of the population well.

Kyle Mercer: Education should match the individual. Right now, we have an educational system that at best serves 10% of the population well. About 10% of kids have minds and bodies that operate well in a traditional educational system. They're able to sit for long periods of time, do repetitive tasks. They're receptive to being fed information and being able to put it back.

There's a large percentage of kids that need a tremendous amount of physical activity and should be in a context that supports that. There are kids that need all sorts of different activities. To really be optimally honoring who they are, we would offer them different settings, with some sports, some crafts, but more of the hands-on activities. There are all sorts of different learning styles that we could be supporting through our educational systems.

Our problem is that we want to generalize education when it really should be specific, and that's what I loved about the model of Summerhill School in Suffolk, England, which I learned about when I was getting my masters in education. Summerhill is a model of a free educational context, where kids gravitate to their own learning.

Home schooling certainly has some of those elements, and there are some kids that it would be really appropriate to home school. But home schooling is also dependent on the parents and who is doing the education, whether that's a fit for them.

Ultimately, I think there's no way to generalize about education. The real question is, "What really serves this child?" Rather than a child serving and being beholden to some system.

Karen Tolchin: It seems as if the madness over standardized testing—with "teaching to the test"—is really a symptom of us trying to make every child fit the same mold, and make every school fit, and that's one of the reasons it's been such a failure.

66

Kyle Mercer:	That's the problem with standardizing education: You end up having education that's good for about 10% of the population. It's a big sacrifice and the implication is, there's a certain kind of kid that is the right kind of kid and then everybody else needs to be drugged and manipulated and have their spirits broken to fit into a certain context.
Karen Tolchin:	When you were talking about the kind of young minds and bodies that need to move a lot, I was thinking of the rise in ADHD and ADD diagnoses. Do you think that could be another symptom of what you're talking about?
Kyle Mercer:	Well, there's some of that and then there's some other things too. I read a study that compared Ritalin to physical activity and found that there is almost equal benefit to four hours of physical activity a day as to taking Ritalin.
	I think a lot of ADHD comes from parents that are totally neurotic and busy and have activity. In my experience, one of the indicators that creates ADHD is having super high expectations, and where there are super high expectations, we can never meet them. So we're jumping from one task to another, trying to do enough to be okay.
Karen Tolchin:	Another symptom of the modern era.
Kyle Mercer:	There's also the case of dyslexia. Dyslexia seems to create really brilliant minds. There are a lot of extremely successful people that are dyslexic. I think it's just all these different kinds of minds, back before standardized education, they saw that different people were different. Some learn this well, some learn that well.

Karen Tolchin:	There's a lot of talk nowadays about what if anything is actually "neuro-typical," particularly in conversations about the rise in diagnoses of autism.
Kyle Mercer:	There are so many different factors, including environmental factors, at work. There are so many different things going on, it's very hard to generalize about it. Again, the question becomes, "What best serves these different kind of thinkers?" They have a tremendous amount to contribute.
	I heard a theory that I don't necessarily agree with, but I like the direction it takes. It said, we're being so controlling as parents, that we are evolving children who refuse to fit the mold. Nature is giving us a bunch of autistic and ADD kids, because they won't submit.
Karen Tolchin:	They're blocking us all out, basically.
Kyle Mercer:	That's right. "We're not going to play your game."
Karen Tolchin:	That would make so much sense.
Kyle Mercer:	Look, fifty years ago, you only got abandoned by one parent. The father went off to work, and you still had the other parent all the time. Now, many kids are essentially being abandoned by both parents as they go off to work. For Americans, that's often a sixty hour work week, so there's just no balance. From the coaching work that I do, I see that this abandonment has huge repercussions. Huge emotional pain comes out in behavior that's reflecting that.
	Whatever dysfunction is going on in all of these homes, it then comes out in the children,

especially when it's not being processed or worked on by the parents. The kids' behaviors mirror what's going on in their homes. There are just so many different factors, and our society has become so dysfunctional around children. Plus, the subject here is **Stop Parenting**. All this parenting is making our kids crazy, and some of the parenting things that we've talked about around creating narcissistic kids ... Yes! Exactly. It's why it's so important to change these patterns around parenting, because we're creating crazy kids! We're passing on our neuroses to our children, and it's happening earlier and earlier.

Karen Tolchin: At the same time, as parents, I think we're going crazier and crazier ourselves.

Kyle Mercer: Exactly, and it's being transferred and it's generational, so we're making our children crazier. Then you can add technology and the speed of life. There's so many factors that go into this, it's hard to nail one down. The question becomes, "How do we help people get back on the healthy path?"

The Big Fat Talk

Kyle and I begin having two sets of calls every week as we embark on this project: my normal coaching call and a book call. Our coaching calls very quickly reveal themselves to be almost indistinguishable from our book calls, so I begin taping both. I'm struggling more than ever with Charlie, who is becoming increasingly oppositional and defiant with me, and I'm trying harder and harder to control the situation—also known as the worst approach. My favorite moment of the day, "bedtime stories," has devolved into a nightly judo match, from which I often walk away bruised and miserable. I'm feeling exhausted and depressed, and my lifelong struggle with low self-esteem is kicking into high gear again.

What follows is meant to be a private coaching call, and it's a doozy. I fight Kyle at every turn, but he won't back down. I believe the conversation shows how very tough **Stop Parenting** has been for me to grasp, both as a philosophy and as a practice.

Karen Tolchin: I've been feeling especially lousy, and really beating up on myself lately, especially about my excess weight. Why am I not more disciplined? Why am I not taking better care of myself? Why don't I have more pride in my appearance? That kind of thing. That would be the nice version. "Gee, you're a big fat fatty" would be the not nice version. I'm flunking blood tests because of my excess weight. It's baby weight, but my baby is six years old.

What's funny is that, when I'm trying to end the day with a lovely bedtime story moment with Charlie, he'll often say the same thing horrible things to me that I'm saying to myself. "Big fat mama!" He'll dive-bomb my stomach and knock the book off the bed. I tell him, "That's not a word that makes people feel good."

Kyle Mercer:	There's that little parenting thing, right?
Karen Tolchin:	Oh, really? Tell me.
Kyle Mercer:	When you say, "That's not a word that makes people feel good," it's preachy and condescending.
Karen Tolchin:	But I feel as if I should respond, especially if he's talking about someone else. Last night, he said it about a friend from school. He said, "Joe's really fat."
Kyle Mercer:	Well, is Joe fat?
Karen Tolchin:	No, he's big. He's tall and big-boned, like a Great Dane puppy, but I don't think he's fat. On the other hand, I know that I'm truly overweight, and Charlie will make a lot of comments about my stomach.
Kyle Mercer:	That's because he gets traction talking about it. Fat is a trigger to get traction with you because he's getting a lot of power.
Karen Tolchin:	This is one of those areas where I'm a little confused because I want him to see it's something that makes me walk away. I want him to see a consequence. "Oh. I thought we were having a good time playing together, but if you're going

to start the name-calling, I'm going into another room."

Kyle Mercer: There's subtlety in this, but the first thing is, he will persist in anything that gets you triggered because it gives him power. He's really supporting and helping you. Probably the best answer to "You're fat!" is "Thank you."

Karen Tolchin: Doesn't that teach him that he should go up and down the countryside, telling people they're fat?

Kyle Mercer: He's probably not going to get a very good reaction out there in the world if he does that.

Karen Tolchin: So, I'm not allowed to give him the same negative reaction that the world's going to give him?

Kyle Mercer: He's triggering you that you've got something to heal. He's totally supporting you in getting healed, right? You can use Inquiry Method to find out more about it. Should we do that?

Karen Tolchin: Okay.

Kyle Mercer: Let's role play. I'm a little fat, so you can call me fat. You be Charlie.

Karen Tolchin: "You have a big, fat belly."

Kyle Mercer: "I do, I do. That is so true."

Karen Tolchin: "How come you're so fat?"

Kyle Mercer: "Because I eat a lot."

Karen Tolchin: "Why do you eat a lot?"

Kyle Mercer: "Well, that's a really good question. I think it's because sometimes I feel insecure or I feel empty and so I try to fill it up with food, but it doesn't really work very well."

Karen Tolchin: "Well, I just think you're fat like a whale."

72

Kyle Mercer:	"Well, whales are bigger and have a lot of fat. It's a different kind of fat, so I don't know if I'm fat like a whale, but I'm certainly fat like me."
Karen Tolchin:	Okay, we can stop. I definitely see there's no power in this for Charlie. This would get boring pretty fast for him.
Kyle Mercer:	There isn't any power in it for him, and you're being really authentic with him, right?
Karen Tolchin:	Mm-hmm (affirmative), right.
Kyle Mercer:	Imagine if he were to copy you. If you made an observation and said, "Charlie, you seem angry right now," he might say, "I'm not angry. It's not nice to say that to people, you bitch." Then you might say, "When you said, 'Bitch,' it sounded angry." "Hey, I'm not angry. How dare you!" he could say.
Karen Tolchin:	Okay, so Charlie is allowed to feel and say whatever he feels like feeling and saying?
Kyle Mercer:	"Allowed to"? Even that concept triggers me. "He's *allowed* to." What does that even mean? "Allowed to." He *does* say whatever he says.
	When you're totally clean with it, and he's running around going, "You're fat, you're fat, you're fat," you might say, "Hey, Charlie, could you take that someplace else? It's too noisy for me here." Then he won't say it anymore.
	He doesn't say, "Mom, you've got two ears." If you were only supposed to have one ear and you had two, and he said, "You have two ears," you wouldn't say, "Don't say I have two ears!" Right? He's making an observation, and it's true.

Karen Tolchin:	Here's where I'm confused. I am trying to be authentic with him. I'm trying to speak to him in a normal, respectful voice, but if he says something hurtful to me, I want to be able to say, "Ouch!"
Kyle Mercer:	But that's just it: The thing he said is not hurtful.
Karen Tolchin:	I don't agree. If he says, "You're fat. You're ugly. I hate you," he is doing it for effect, and the effect he's after is to hurt me. I certainly want to be smarter than he is, I want to outsmart him and I see what you're saying about, "Don't let him get any traction," but—
Kyle Mercer:	I'm not talking about outsmarting him. You *can't* outsmart him. I'm just talking about truth. It comes back to truth, all right? I could say, "It's really interesting when you say that. I find that … " Let's see. "When you say that, I react to it in a way that I create hurt." He's not hurting you, right?
Karen Tolchin:	He's not?
Kyle Mercer:	If he said, "You have blue hair. I hate your blue hair," you'd go, "What?" Right? "I don't have blue hair." "You've got blue hair." "You're hurting my feelings saying I have blue hair." You wouldn't do it, right?
Karen Tolchin:	Am I feeling hurt because he's saying a negative perception of my body that I share?
Kyle Mercer:	It's the only reason that bothers you, and why does he pick that? *Because it bothers you.* He wants to get traction with you. Until you're okay with your fatness or have addressed it, he's just the one reminding you to get back on your path.
Karen Tolchin :	I'm not allowed to tell him when he's hurting me?

Kyle Mercer:	He's *not* hurting you! That's your misperception. *You're being hurt.*
Karen Tolchin:	But I can't even tell my child when what he's saying is painful for me to hear?
Kyle Mercer:	You're stating it in the wrong... I'm trying to help you to an understanding. I'm saying the whole universe is going to reflect to you what you need to do to get back on the path of joy. Pain, hurt, anger, all this stuff is the universe gleefully, joyfully, lovingly trying to help you get back on the path that everything is just love and joy. It's, every time you start stepping off the path of love and joy, the universe says or does something to say, "That hurts to have that thought or to have that approach or to be doing what you're doing. That hurts. Get back on the path of love and joy."
	The more you push into that false thing, the more the universe lovingly creates pain. It says, "No, no. You're going in the wrong direction." For instance, if I had the thought that I'm fat and it hurts, that's the universe saying, "Don't think that." Right? Or, if you think, "Nobody loves me," and it hurts, the universe is saying, "Hurtful thought. Stop thinking that." If your son is saying, "You're fat," and it creates pain, you know you're out of alignment somewhere.
Karen Tolchin:	This is so hard for me. Why is this so hard?
Kyle Mercer:	Maybe the whole message from your son is, "Mom, you're not taking care of your body and I want you to be around forever." Maybe that's what he's saying or else what the universe is saying through him. It's a loving message that there's something out of balance. It might be great to

75

advise him to run around singing, "You're fat," until you lose as many pounds as you want to lose. Then, you say, "I'm exactly the way that I want to be." If he still says, "No, you're fat," you could say, "Okay, but I'm exactly the way that I want to be." He would have no traction left. It's only you that's creating the pain, the hurt of it. He's not being hurtful. He's just supporting you by pointing out your pain.

Karen Tolchin: I think I'm beginning to grasp this, but here's where I think I'm confused. What if we go to a playground together and Charlie says to another mom on the playground, "You're big and fat like a whale," and she bursts into tears and says, "What a horrible little boy," and walks away?

Kyle Mercer: What does that say about you if she says, "What a horrible little boy?"

Karen Tolchin: Well, no. It's not that, obviously.

Kyle Mercer: It *is* that, actually. It is. What does it say about you if she says, "What a horrible little boy?"

Karen Tolchin: I'm a bad mother.

Kyle Mercer: That's right.

Karen Tolchin: I'm trying to embrace that whole "Bad Mother" thing, but—

Kyle Mercer: Wait, I understand, I know you're trying, but let's stay with this. If Charlie goes out and says, "Hey, lady. You're fat," and she says, "What a horrible little boy. Who's your mother?" He points at you. "That fatso over there," he says.

Karen Tolchin: Oh, it just gets better and better! "That fatso over there."

76

We feel schizophrenic when we get a conditional love message.

Kyle Mercer:	The stranger might say, "That lady's not going to win any awards for Best Mother."
Karen Tolchin:	Here's my sticking point. To look at this fictional stranger's tears, Charlie gets to hear her words and learn from that. He gets to say, "Oh! When I say these words, that makes people miserable. It makes people turn away from me. That's not how I want to be in the world."
Kyle Mercer:	It gives him the opportunity to recognize that, yes.
Karen Tolchin:	I don't see why can't I do the same thing inside our home.
Kyle Mercer:	Well, the difference, there's a total difference between you and everybody else. Well, there's two big differences. One is, *you* actually want to grow spiritually, and you have the perfect support in growing because Charlie has no boundaries and is going to point out every single way that you are not evolved. He is your perfect support mechanism and he will keep yelling it at the top of his lungs as long as it bothers you, until you heal it. He's totally supporting you in being evolved and at peace. That's the first thing.
	The second thing is, you are his mother. My story about primal humanness is this. Imagine that we grew up in a village and then we all had children, right? Let's say we all had teepees, and my children were in my teepee and your children

were in your teepee. Say that my child goes out in the world and does something, does graffiti on somebody else's teepee, right? They're mad at him and scold him, and he comes back and he says, "That lady's mad at me because I did graffiti on her teepee." As his father, I could just ask, "How do you feel about that?" I'm modeling the capacity for acceptance and unconditional love. He's already gotten his lesson out there. He doesn't need to get the lesson from me, too.

Karen Tolchin: I see. Again, as with Henry biting Matthew, it's, "No piling on."

Kyle Mercer: Right. No piling on.

What makes us feel schizophrenic is when we get a conditional love message. Our parents are supposed to love us unconditionally. When they condition the love, they're saying there's no such thing as unconditional love and it doesn't get modeled through them for children to love themselves. There's a difference between love and behavior that needs to be corrected. Conditional love means, "I only love you when you do what I want you to do. I only love you when you don't call me fat." Right?

Karen Tolchin: What would you consider behavior that *does* need to be corrected?

Kyle Mercer: Ideally, all behavior would be corrected by someone other than the parents. In a village, I would want the approval of my uncles, right? If I went on a hunting trip with them and made noise, they would look on me with disapproval, but it wouldn't be my parent. It would just be,

78

"That is not getting respect with us," right? I'd go, "Well, I'd like to correct that." We know this.

If my father looks at me and says, "You jackass" for making noise, all of a sudden it's, "You don't love me." Then it's a quick jump to, "Oh, yeah? I'm going to make all the noise I want." Right? We see that reaction all the time. Charlie's doing it with you. He behaves better with other people, right?

Karen Tolchin: Much better. He's a total sweetheart with just about everyone else on the planet.

Kyle Mercer: That's because he's not looking for uncondi-tional love from everyone else. He's pointing out to you that, "You're not loving me." I don't mean gushy love. Actually, it would be a very quiet love, right? It's just really deep acceptance more than anything. Just love. It's not, "Oh, you're so wonderful." It's not "I just love you to pieces whether you're good or bad." No, it's grounded, peaceful anchoring. From my parents, I want that anchoring love. I want to go home and say, "Oh, I'm grounded. Everything's okay. All right, I'm back to zero. All right, now I can go back out in the world and risk it all again."

Now, I do create boundaries for myself, but I grow first. With your fat, you want to correct it so that you don't have to feel the pain, which means you're avoiding your own issue about it. That's not an appropriate correction, right? You haven't done your work around it. You're still being trig-gered by it.

Now, a different one would be if he is in the room where you're grading papers yelling at the top of his lungs and knocking over your piles of paper. That's different. You say, "Charlie, what I want to do right now is grade papers and I can't do it while you're behaving in that way. It's all right if you want to behave that way, just not in here."

"Tough love" is still totally hooked because the parent is triggered.

That's setting a boundary for yourself, not for him. I'm not saying, "Good boys don't knock over papers." Right?

Karen Tolchin: I wouldn't be saying, "I will love you only if you do this."

Kyle Mercer: That would be conditional love, setting a boundary for *him*, telling *him* what he can and cannot do. It would be better to set a boundary for *yourself*. You're allowed to create the space you want for yourself, especially around your body. There's no reason for him to be dive-bombing your stomach, right?

You can't really create boundaries for what other people do, but you can have certain preferences for what you want to have in your environment right now. It doesn't come across right if it's triggered. He's, "Yeah, it's not really about that. It's just you don't like being called fat." Right? It's

THE BIG FAT TALK

different and it's subtle, but it's because it's an emotional trigger and not just a preference.

Karen Tolchin: This is so helpful because—and I know this is shocking—I think I have some work left to do here. This is a piece of **Stop Parenting** that I really haven't been able to grasp.

Kyle Mercer: This is why **Stop Parenting** is a self-actualization: because you can't do it without cleaning up your own baggage. A child always wants to control the source of nourishment, and you're Charlie's source of nourishment. If he can find a way to hook you and keep your attention, it's like gold. You're always going to have to grow around your child because he's always going to find a new way to hook you. You just have to get unhook-able. People say, "Well, I'm going to become tough, a tough love parent." I say, "That's fine, but tough love's totally hooked."

Karen Tolchin: How is tough love "totally hooked"?

Kyle Mercer: With tough love, the parent is too emotional about it. It's like, "I'm doing something to shape you into what you're supposed to be." There's another subtlety here, but some kids just need to know there are boundaries to be safe. That's a whole other subtlety, but my experience is, this happens very young and then we don't need to rebel. Rebellion requires authority, right?

You can tell how controlling you're being in a relationship by how much resistance you're encountering.

Karen Tolchin: Right.

Kyle Mercer: If we have no authority, there's nothing to rebel against. Rebellion is created by authority. You can tell how controlling you're being in a relationship by how much resistance you're encountering. When I'm a parent who uses authority, "Do this. Don't do that," and you have that with Charlie all the time, when you say, "Don't call me fat," etc., he perceives that as authority. "Aha! Authority. I'm going to rebel against it."

When you have no authority, when calling you fat is not a rebellion, he'll stop. If you say, "Don't say blue," Charlie's going to go, "Blue. Blue. Blue. Blue." Right?

Karen Tolchin: He's been very oppositional with me.

Kyle Mercer: Once you realize this, you can actually manipulate him all over the place if you want. I don't recommend it, but you can manipulate him just by channeling his rebellion, especially at this age. He won't be able to pick it up. You can tell him anything's rebellion and get him to do it.

Karen Tolchin: "Boy, it would really make me mad if you brushed your teeth."

Kyle Mercer: That's it. Issue a decree: "I've decided there'll be no more teeth brushing."

Karen Tolchin:	"Oh, yeah?" he'd say. "Here I go."
Kyle Mercer:	"I'm going to hide a toothbrush under my mattress! I'm going to do whatever I want…"
	That's why Charlie is such an amazing teacher. He's going to point out any resistances you have, because he's trying to get traction with you. Then you can do your own work and get clean.
Karen Tolchin:	This is so hard for me. I've always been told that I'm too sensitive, and now that sensitivity is interfering in my relationship with my son. I really need to get a thicker skin.

Your resistance is helping you find the untilled parts of your soul.

Kyle Mercer:	It's actually *not* about creating armor or protection, it's the opposite direction. We are *all* that sensitive. Some people are very armored to it, but it also makes them blind. As we grow, we tend to get more sensitive, in fact. That sensitivity is just awareness. It doesn't necessarily have to be reactivity.
	The direction of growth is becoming transparent to your points of resistance. If you're sensitive, if you're having a reaction to it, it means you're having an attachment or some area of density within your being: emotional pain, ego, those kinds of things. It's really there to serve you when that resistance comes up in view, because

it's helping you find those untilled parts of your soul. It's tilling your soil. Then you can say, "Oh, wow, isn't that interesting? I've got some resistance around this..."

As you become transparent to your energy, it just flows through you. You can be aware of it without it causing you trouble. The problem is when it sticks. It's not a problem that you're too sensitive to it, because the other direction is equally problematic. It's acquiring a sort of armor, which would be much more like Tom's approach, right? The armor doesn't allow any evolution.

Karen Tolchin: It makes it much harder, yes.

Kyle Mercer: You just want to become more transparent, so you can say, "Oh, I'm resisting the negativity." When you release the energy, your resistance to it, it just flows through and it doesn't land. That's exactly the whole thing about this **Stop Parenting** perspective. Anything that you're sensitive about your child, and there's some density, it creates traction and they're drawn to keep on creating that tension in you, because it gives them power. Maybe they're even trying to refine you, so that you can be fully the parent that they want, not having those resistances.

It's like the universe is totally filling up, to help you clean that out.

Karen Tolchin: It sounds as if I should thank the universe, but I'm not quite there yet.

Becoming transparent to my own energy around parenting… I can feel the wisdom in what you're saying, but I'm still a little bit unclear, no pun intended, about what that would look like for me.

Kyle Mercer: Let's say I'm at the swimming pool, and I've got energy around my child being hurt. Who knows what that's about? It could be about, "A good parent wouldn't let their child get hurt," or it could be about, "What will people think?" It could be about, "That child's so reckless," or whatever it is.

I see my child running at the pool. I yell, "Don't run at the pool!" That's totally engaging with that energy, right?

What I would do is, I would feel my resistance to that, and I would get transparent about it, and then I would let it go. I'd just feel all the energy I had in my being around their running, and I would be with that feeling, just like we're letting go of emotional pain. I'd be with that feeling, and I'd let it go. I'd fly into that storm, and just allow what's happening.

Karen Tolchin: Okay, except that you're not supposed to run at the pool. What if your instinct to holler at your child is coming from a good place? A protective place?

Kyle Mercer: What would be important about not running at the pool?

Karen Tolchin: He could fall and crack his head open on the concrete and die. And then I would never recover from the loss. A Greek tragedy, all because I didn't say, "Stop running!"

Kyle Mercer: Okay, great. Look at the damage that you're doing to your *relationship* and your *fun at the pool*, when your whole energy is sitting there focused on all that. Feel that energy with Charlie, sit with it for a moment. "No running at the pool!" Charlie will have your complete attention and engagement just by walking really quickly, just finding that limit.

Karen Tolchin: It's as if you've got secret cameras in our house.

Kyle Mercer: I don't need secret cameras. All kids do this. This is the whole parenting thing. When you've got some of that density, for whatever reason, they want to point it out. They love to play with that energy.

One of the reasons Henry is so naturally himself is that he discovered all those limits on his own. The great thing about the pool nowadays is, they've got somebody else to yell at them.

Karen Tolchin: Thank God. It's one place I can relax and know the world really will do the teaching. Thank God for lifeguards.

Stop Parenting is a self-actualization process. You can't do it without cleaning up your own baggage.

Kyle Mercer: Yeah, but it's ridiculous anyway. I don't imagine that the "running at the pool" deaths are very high, right?

Karen Tolchin: I don't know.

Kyle Mercer:	I would expect the statistics would be pretty low, although you might say that's because there are so many moms running around, policing the situation.
Karen Tolchin:	Right, it's because we hold a constant vigil.
Kyle Mercer:	If moms weren't policing, there'd be millions of "running at the pool" deaths!
Karen Tolchin:	Exactly! You know, we actually hosted Charlie's sixth birthday party at a water park yesterday.
Kyle Mercer:	Oh, that's perfect.
Karen Tolchin:	We learned early on that it's a great venue for little kids. They get covered in cake and frosting, and then it all gets hosed off. Anyway, I'm pretty sure I said, "No running" at least five times. I also reapplied his sunscreen three times but completely neglected to put any on myself. And then got a sunburn. Which is a perfect metaphor for modern parenting.
Kyle Mercer:	These are all kind of over-hyperprotective things that engage that resistant quality, that quality children have for seeking out density in your soul, right? Your resistance right now, that you're noticing everywhere you look, is negativity. You're just bathed in a sea of negativity. In that perfect universe, it's so supportive of you getting over it.
Karen Tolchin:	Getting over what? My distaste for negativity?
Kyle Mercer:	Yeah, your resistance to negativity.
Karen Tolchin:	Okay, so how do I surrender my resistance to negativity?

Kyle Mercer: I don't know if I've told you the story about my employee, but she had a mother that was very negative, and she was going to go see her. I said, "Let's try something totally different." Mom was totally negative about things like, "Oh, I have no friends, I'm sick, I'm probably going to die," all this kind of stuff.

The daughter would always go there and try to talk her out of it. "No, mom, you're fine. You're actually pretty healthy for your age. Things are okay," blah, blah, blah, all this kind of positivity, trying to instill this positivity in Mom.

Mom never felt as if she was getting heard. What I said is, "Go with it. When your mom says, 'I'm so sick,' say 'Yeah, Mom, I can tell you're really kind of circling the drain,' or 'Yeah, you're so unhealthy.'" When the mother said, "Oh, I think I'm going to die pretty soon," the daughter said, "Yeah, I can see that. Yeah, you probably don't have too much longer." Well, finally, the mother got heard, so she starting defending herself! She got sort of indignant and said, "Well, I'm not dead yet." She started standing up for herself.

Once the mother got heard, she didn't have to keep insisting on all of it. In fact, she started to change her attitude.

Karen Tolchin: It's ironic. By surrendering, the daughter finally heard what she wanted to hear from her mother all along. A little positivity.

I've been trying to listen to Charlie, and let him get out the negativity. When I ask about his day, and he says it was terrible, I say, "Oh, I'm sorry to hear that. What happened? What made it terrible?" He'll say, "My friends all chopped my head off." Then I'll say, "Oh, that's so interesting."

Kyle Mercer: Wait—but it's *not* interesting.

Karen Tolchin: It's not?

Kyle Mercer: No, it's totally boring. It's a bunch of made-up stuff. I'm not interested in that. I'd be totally bored by that. I'd have no interest in that conversation whatsoever. Do you really have an interest in that conversation? "How was your day?"

Karen Tolchin: Well, I want to know why he's so interested in blood and guts, and so I've been trying to inquire into it and let him talk more about it in the same way that you described...

Kyle Mercer: No, the negative talk is pushing your buttons, so he's really interested in it. He's getting you to behave un-authentically. Again, I can hear it; every time you start talking to Charlie about something and you have tension about it, you get this uplifting lilt in your voice. Do you know how you kind of raise that pitch of your voice?

Karen Tolchin: I do?

Kyle Mercer: Yeah, that's ... Let's just start with that being a lie, every time. It's the opposite of what you're feeling.

Karen Tolchin If I hear my own voice go up, then it's a lie. Okay. But then, how do I talk to my child about his day?

Kyle Mercer: Part of it ... What he's resisting is that you're burrowing into his life.

I had a mother who was needy of my well-being. She attached herself to my well-being.

When I got home from school, she would ask me how my day was. If I started sharing it with her, she'd get co-dependent around it. I'd say, "I like this girl, and she didn't talk to me." She'd say, "Oh, sweetie, you'll find the girl of your dreams someday. They just don't recognize how wonderful you are," all this kind of stuff, which didn't feel good.

If I didn't want to talk about it, she'd want to burrow in and get in there and penetrate my reserve. I didn't have a safe place for my stuff.

I think Charlie's pushback is partly because you so want to get into his space. I would just stop asking him how his day was altogether. He's not giving you anything anyway.

Karen Tolchin: That's an interesting idea. There's absolutely nothing authentic that comes out of those conversations.

Turtles All the Way Down

I*n this conversation, Kyle demonstrates—yet again—how **Stop Parenting** is really a call for parents to tend to their own gardens. I am beginning to see this every day. When I'm feeling grounded and peaceful, I sow a much different crop in my family. I am beginning to believe that my relationship with my child is actually a great opportunity to develop an authentic spiritual practice—not as a hobby or a curiosity, but as a way of moving through the world and living my life. Never have I been more challenged to maintain my inner peace, and I'm starting to see that Charlie is the perfect Zen master for me. He'll throw everything he can at me until I get good and balanced.*

Karen Tolchin:	So, I have a "Mama's fat" update for you. Charlie was doing the whole "Mama's got a great, big, fat belly. Chicken Fat Mama. Mama Chicken, Mama fat…" I don't really know how chickens got involved, but suddenly there were chickens…
	After our last coaching call conversation, I stopped feeling hurt about it and stopped trying to shame Charlie for saying "Fat." I decided to just go with it. I said, "Yes, it's true. I'm a big fat mama chicken, hear me cluck cluck cluck!" It just became something totally different.
Kyle Mercer:	How has that changed how he interacts with you about it?

Karen Tolchin:	Oh, we've been interacting incredibly well as a result. There's a different quality to our time together. It's more relaxed and fun, and in the moment. There hasn't been the same intensity around my weight, etc.
Kyle Mercer:	It no longer has any traction with you. That's great. So, what do you want to talk about today?
Karen Tolchin:	I've been meditating on something you said in our last conversation. You said, "You need Charlie to show up for you in a certain way. When he doesn't, it's a problem." I saw how accurate that was, and how very backwards for me as his parent. It's not Charlie's job to show up for me in any particular way.
Kyle Mercer:	That's right.
Karen Tolchin:	I'm also really working on not trying to intervene, if he's having feelings that are negative or inconvenient. Not trying to convince him to feel different. All of that has helped a great deal. Because I want Charlie to be able to just exist and not have to deserve, or show up in a particular way to be loved. I want him to be able to be himself and have that deep acceptance that you've described. But if I've inherited these deeply held beliefs that you have to deserve what you get and that you aren't just okay, then I'm surely going to pass that on.
Kyle Mercer:	These beliefs are, with the best of intentions, of course, passed on. Your parents got it from somewhere, too, right?
Karen Tolchin:	They were both raised by Depression-era parents.

Kyle Mercer:	I see. I was actually noticing some of that in myself. It's like, this very A to B mindset. Henry and I were building a pen for his tortoise, a place for him to live.
Karen Tolchin:	Oh, cool.
Kyle Mercer:	I was just noticing how A to B I was about the process. "Okay, do this, do this, get that done..." I used to build, so I'm going to get the job done. I'm just noticing, Henry is sitting down, hanging out, watching the birds, and I'm thinking, "This job is never going to get done!" I'm so A to B, and he has a totally different approach, partly because he hasn't had a job before, and I've had jobs, so I know, "Oh, you've got to get things done." I just became very aware of that A to B imprint nature expectation I have of myself.
Karen Tolchin:	To be productive, to get the job done means being productive. There's such a high value placed on that in my family as well.
Kyle Mercer:	Yes, and you don't see that in the Amazon.
Karen Tolchin:	No. I gather there isn't a lot of crippling psychiatric anxiety in the Amazon, either, but it's just rampant in our culture. Since our "Fat Mama" talk, which was so hard for me, I've become hyper aware of my boundaries with Charlie. For a long time, I wasn't sure where he stopped and I started, probably because we shared a body for so many months... So, the boundaries have gotten terribly blurred, and that seems to give rise to some trouble.
Kyle Mercer:	There's an underlying principle that needs to be addressed, and that is this: We're always setting

93

boundaries for other people, and that's not acceptable. It's not okay to set a boundary for somebody else. You can set a boundary for yourself, though. In fact, it's important to be able to set boundaries for yourself. That's a whole project in and of itself.

Karen Tolchin: Can you give an example of someone setting a boundary for a child, and damaging him in the process?

Kyle Mercer: Sure. I had depression. I was told that it was wrong to be depressed, that I was supposed to just get over it. It was 180 degrees the wrong direction. Someone finally said, "Dude, you're freaking depressed, let's talk about this." Then, oh, that was such a relief, but until then, I thought there was something wrong with me.

Do you see how I said, "I thought there was something wrong with me"? But I was just depressed. Do you see the difference?

Karen Tolchin: Is it that it wasn't who you are as a person, your identity or your character, but rather how you felt?

Kyle Mercer: I was always told that I was normal, but I was being an idiot to be depressed. I was like, no, wait a minute, let's turn this around. I'm depressed, so how am I going to work with that?

My dad hated that I was depressed and resisted it, and, for a time, it turned me against myself.

Karen Tolchin: Hearing that, it makes sense that a deep acceptance of the child has become the cornerstone of **Stop Parenting**. That is, the number one job of the parent is to see, accept, and love your child, to the best of your ability, and to recognize from the beginning that you are two different people. Without that, I mean, from what you're describing in your own experience, even with a pretty forward-thinking dad... To be turned against yourself would not be good.

Kyle Mercer: Let me just emphasize something, because the ultimate key is this: You can only do this with your child to the level to which you've done it to yourself. If we're really going to tell the truth, then **Stop Parenting and Get Your Act Together** should be the title of this book.

Karen Tolchin: Everything really does connect, because, even in our coaching calls about adult relationships, what you said to me that was so powerful, and that no one had said to me before is, "If you have a problem with the other person, it's you." Like, whatever you're seeing in the other person that's infuriating you, whatever's triggering you, that you're attributing to the other person as *his* flaw...

If you are happy and grounded in life, your kids will be, too.

Kyle Mercer: That's right.

Karen Tolchin: This is really about *you*. In a fundamental respect, this looking at yourself, this getting knowledge about yourself and cultivating a deep acceptance of yourself is the prerequisite to having a

95

sound relationship with *anyone*, be it, spouse, parent, or child.

Kyle Mercer: That's right. Here's another key question. Would you want anyone treating you the way you treat yourself?

Karen Tolchin: For most people, I think the answer would be, "Heck no!" We're all much harder on ourselves than we are on others.

Kyle Mercer: Then we end up treating our children probably 80% of how we treat ourselves.

Karen Tolchin: It's the ego that says, "My child is an extension of me." Well, if you're beating yourself up, then you're going to beat your kid up, too.

Kyle Mercer: That's right, and the ultimate irony is that the way you treat yourself is how you were treated by your parents.

Karen Tolchin: This is deeply cyclical.

Kyle Mercer: Yes. It's turtles all the way down.

Karen Tolchin: Turtles? Are we talking about Henry's tortoise again?

Kyle Mercer: No, no. Haven't I shared this with you yet? It might be my favorite joke. This student goes to his teacher, and he goes, "Teacher, what holds the world up?" The teacher says, "There's this huge turtle, and the world rests on its back." The student says, "What does the turtle rest on?" The teacher says, "There's another turtle." So the student asks, "Okay, but what does *that* turtle rest on?" The teacher says, "It's turtles all the way down!" [In his book *A Brief History of Time*,

Stephen Hawking attributes this anecdote to Bertrand Russell.]

If you want your kids to be decent, be decent. If you want your kids to be happy people, be happy, but authentically happy.

Karen Tolchin: Oh my God, yes. "Turtles all the way down!" In the case of repeating your own parenting, it could go down centuries and centuries, and millennia… Yes, it's endless turtles!

Kyle Mercer: That's right, except for this: Our contemporary approach is a function of western civilization. It's *not* a function of being human.

Karen Tolchin: Is there an alternative model you could share?

Kyle Mercer: I would say my biggest influence around this is a book I read called *Hanta Yo* by Ruth Beebe Hill, which was about the Lakota Sioux Indians. Just their way of being in the world and parenting.

The other important truth is, your kids are going to turn out just like you, no matter what you say or do.

Karen Tolchin: The news just gets worse and worse.

Kyle Mercer: If you want them to be decent, be decent. If you want your kids to be happy people, be happy! But *authentically* happy. Let's throw out our definition of success as having a sixty-hour job, and

97

seeing your children four hours a week. And teaching our children that's the definition of success.

Karen Tolchin: Okay, so what is genuine success? Or authentic happiness? If I want to model that for my child.

Kyle Mercer: The first thing is, don't model, just be. What I'm discovering is that joy and bliss are the ground of being. Love is the underpinning of everything. Now, if I want to get particular, I can say, "Well, love is only things that I love. I only love that person," or, "I'm only going to be happy when this person loves me." Or, "I only like Ferraris. I'll experience love when I see a Ferrari. It's the only way that you can shape metal and 4 wheels, that makes me happy."

Or else you can say, "Wow! Metal! Four wheels. It goes vroom! That's cool!" You can say, "Look, a rock!" That's what kids do naturally, right? "Look, a rock!"

Your kids are going to turn out just like you, no matter what you say or do.

Karen Tolchin: It's actually my favorite thing about being with a little kid every day. I had forgotten how exciting the simplest things can be.

Kyle Mercer: "It's shaped like a pointy thing. It looks like a mountain," or whatever. It's as if everything makes a kid happy. You take a kid to Paris and he'll say, "Look at this gravel in the driveway!" I want to say, "I don't get it, it's just like the gravel we have back home." My kid says, "I know. Isn't it great?"

Karen Tolchin: As a parent, I would say, "Why did I spend all this money for us to be in Paris? Check out the Seine, Notre Dame, anything we don't have at home!"

Kyle Mercer: Why not just say, "This is great gravel. Cool." We might as well get into it with our kids, right?

Karen Tolchin: It actually shows how arrogant we are in assuming we need to teach our kids what to love, what to enjoy.

Kyle Mercer: It's awesome gravel! They don't need us to tell them. Everything is love, and then getting more practical, say, "Well, why not pick an easier object of love?" That's why Jesus is so popular. "I'm going to hang a picture of him on the wall. I'm just going to love the heck out of that Jesus." It's, "Ah! Love! I love Jesus. He's great. Amazing. Every time I think of Jesus I just feel love. Great, good job," right?

That's brilliant. It's portable. It takes up no room and luggage. All I need is my love for Jesus, right?

Karen Tolchin: Right. I love it. I can't believe you're suggesting that the secret of Jesus' success is that he makes people feel good. If we ever go on a book tour together, I'm investing in a bulletproof vest.

Kyle Mercer: You can simplify it even more. How about just love myself? "I'm fantastic. What a miracle. Look, I can walk around. It's unbelievable! How does this happen? I'm alive." They took you from

99

non-existence and said, "Hey, would you like to try existence?" You'd say, "Yes." "Not everything's going to go your way." You'd say, "Who cares? Look out. Let's give it a try!" That's the deal. Every time you wake up you go from non-existence to existence. It's, "Cool. What's happening today?" Are you going to get up and feel insecure about what's happening today?

Karen Tolchin: No?

Kyle Mercer: No. It's "Wow. This is intense. I'm alive." That's the potentiality, and then ultimately, once you recognize that everything is love, you say, "Wow! The ground of being is love. I am love." Then, instead of looking for it, you just recognize, "I am love." That is really simple.

Ultimately, we're just playing on the surface here, and the more you open up to that, the more it's just amazing. The universe responds to you. It's just, "Oh, yes. Absolutely. Let's try this on."

Karen Tolchin: You've said in the past that at one point in time, you were quite miserable. Have you found an increase in your own happiness just by simplifying your life and focusing on love?

Kyle Mercer: Whatever it is, it's just coming through me more and more. I have everything I need. Sometimes I can get confused about that and say to myself, "Listen. Wow, I really need that fancy car over there." Or whatever. Then I wonder, "Do I need that? I already have that." Wanting is the opposite of having, right? As soon as I want something, I don't have it. I want approval. If you want approval, you don't have approval.

If you say, "I lack happiness. I'm missing something. I don't have it." Do you have happiness? You want to *be* happy, but why don't you just *have* happy?

Karen Tolchin: If you just *have happy*, you're already there.

How to Talk to My Own Child

Before I became a parent, it never occurred to me that talking to my child would be fraught with so much potential hazard. After all, I'm a classic extrovert: I like talking with most people. My brother used to laugh every time he picked me up at the airport just in time to hear me wrapping up an intimate conversation with a stranger. I'd be saying something like, "Good luck with your gallbladder surgery!" or "I hope you and your husband find a way to regain the trust!" I've always believed that it's one of life's great pleasures to connect with others through story. But now I'm tongue-tied and stymied with the one person I want to know better than anyone else on the planet: my son.

As far as stories go, Kyle has me rethinking the power of story in my life. I've seen how it can be a force for good, but now I'm seeing how it can also be a force for ill. For instance, I've been spinning one heck of a self-pitying tale in my own head about how I just can't seem to get anything right with Charlie. Just when I'm whooping for joy, thinking we've made it safely beyond the days of the "Big Fat Mama" conversation, I see that we're somewhere even more distressing.

Charlie has become smitten with all things war-related. He's as taken with death, destruction, and dismemberment as I was with dolls at his age. I understand that boys tend to gravitate towards war play, but the negativity seems excessive.

"How was school?" I ask Charlie every afternoon.

"Terrible!" he says, even though I just watched him hug three of his best friends and skip—yes, skip!—all the way from his classroom to the car.

"What made it terrible?" I hear myself say, almost against my own will.

"Well, Connor chopped my head off, and so I cut his arm off, and then there was

blood everywhere," he says. "And poop, lots of poop!"

This might seem like a funny vignette, but when you get a deluge of mutilation and poop talk for hours every day, just when you're trying mightily to accentuate the positive in your own life… Well, it can set a person's teeth on edge. School has just let out for the summer, so at our house, it's basically all war and poop talk, all the time. My teeth are wearing down to jagged nubs.

"Honey, you were born into a family of pacifists," I say lamely as Charlie pretends to gut me for the fortieth time that day. "Wouldn't you rather play a nice game of Greenpeace?" I feel like Stewie's mom in **Family Guy**, except that I'm not blissfully unaware of my warlike creation.

We're on vacation in Vermont with extended family. I've been waiting for this moment all year, anticipating the cool mountain air, the farmers markets, the waterfalls and covered bridges. But in reality, I'm feeling tired and stressed, like a burnt-out cruise director. The more family members who are present, the harder it is for me to remain calm, grounded, and authentic—mostly because I feel compelled to balance everyone's competing needs, interests, and feelings. Even with all the sweet mountain pleasures that abound in Vermont, I end up imagining that any given moment, at least one person is disappointed in me.

For the first time, I totally get why so many mothers throughout history have been sent away for a "rest cure." I lock myself in an upstairs bedroom and place a call to Kyle, who listens with compassion and then speaks with his trademark candor. He shows me how my actions

*are amplifying the war talk with Charlie. Through role-play, Kyle mod-
els a different way of relating to my son. He even uses a potent guided
meditation technique on "Charlie"—i.e., me taking the Charlie part in
our role-play—and I'm awed by the change. Kyle has used this technique with me (the real me) in many a coaching call. I don't know why
it has never occurred to me to offer it to my son.*

Karen Tolchin: I'm in the soup again, Kyle.

Kyle Mercer: Great! Tell me about it.

Karen Tolchin: There's a lot going on, but the most vexing piece of it involves Charlie. I'm having a lot of trouble just talking to him again. It's not the "big fat mama" stuff anymore, thank the good Lord, but it's a lot of random brutality talk. My goal is to spend more one-on-one time with my kid, but after a few minutes of this I feel like running for the hills.

        I've been comparing notes with other moms, and I think I might not be alone in this. Could you outline for me, and maybe for other parents who are equally flummoxed, just how to talk to children about their day?

Kyle Mercer: This is a recurring theme for us. "What do I talk to my child about?" This is a total misconception. You don't need to. You really don't. It's kind of like what Harry Truman said: "The best way to advise your children is ask them what they want to do, and advise them to do it." If you are willing to be patient, and not attached to things, they will come to you eventually and ask.

        If you stop meddling in your kid's life and stop needing to control and manage him and all of that kind of stuff, there's just not that much to say.

104

You're just two people living your lives. If you're patient, at some point, even though you've conditioned them *not* to talk to you about anything by your meddling, at some point they will get to a place where they don't know what to do. Because you've been silent and you've been patient, they actually say, "Mom, I don't know how to do my math problem. I don't know how to do math." Your tendency then will be to say, "Oh, great! I've been bottling it all up so I'll gush on you and tell you all about what I think about math, what I've been thinking about your problem with math."

Just stop.

Being inauthentic with our children causes damage.

Karen Tolchin: Just stop? Like, say nothing?

Kyle Mercer: No, you just need to use Inquiry at this point. All you need to say is, "What do you need?" They might say, "Well, I need help." "What kind of help would you like?" "I don't know how to do this problem." "What would you like me to do?" "I want you to sit down and do this problem with me." "Okay, how would I do it?" "I want you to give me the answer." You could write down the answer and then just stop there, and then they could say, "How'd you get that answer?" You say, "Here, I'll show you."

The goal is to have your child lead his own Inquiry about how to get what he needs.

The more you do that, the more they'll have a tendency to start to come to you. The more you meddle, the more they'll resist you and the less they can actually use your wisdom and contribution and what you have to offer.

Karen Tolchin: Okay, wonderful. Except that for me and for many other parents that's going to leave a great big gaping silence in the day. Especially during summer vacations.

Kyle Mercer: It'll give you time to meditate.

Karen Tolchin: You know, I *have* always wanted to take up golf…

Kyle Mercer: Exactly! Take up golf, read a book…

Karen Tolchin: In all seriousness, I'm not sure this will solve the problem. I want to connect with Charlie, but all he seems to want to talk about is blood and gore.

Kyle Mercer: I *am* being serious. Read a book. Play golf. Meditate.

The authentic thing about Charlie coming home and telling about how he got his head chopped off at school is that it's totally boring and uninteresting for you. Why would you want to have that conversation with him day after day?

Karen Tolchin: That's just it: I don't. I hate it.

Kyle Mercer: Of course you do. It's ridiculous.

Charlie's a master. In a way, you could even consider what he's doing as irony. He's just saying to you, "I don't want to talk about my day. I don't want to have your nose in my day so I'm going

106

to tell you some garbage and I can't believe you keep engaging me like I'm spewing something valuable. I'm telling you I don't want to relate about my day."

That seems like such a clear message from him. If you asked one of your coworkers or Tom, "How was your day?" and they said, "I got my brains blown out and I had a car wreck and I died three times," you'd be like, "Whatever dude." You would walk away.

Karen Tolchin: It seems as though a lot of the wisdom in **Stop Parenting** hinges on getting our focus off the child. That's extra hard for my generation of parents, the helicopter set. We are hyper-focused on our kids.

Kyle Mercer: Don't feed into it. Don't say anything. If he presses you about why, all of a sudden, you're not engaging him about his day, you can just say, "I just didn't find it very fun to ask you how your day was." If he asks why not, say, "What would be fun for me is to hear what really happened during your day." Then he might say, "Oh, I don't want to tell you." Then you could say, "Great. That's fine."

I suspect that at this point, Charlie might say, "Well, I did do this today." Then you could say, "What was that like for you?"

Here's the point: You're way too embroiled and attached to Charlie's day. It's like, all of a sudden if he tells you he had a hard time, you're going to be on the phone with the teacher, or put him in art therapy or something.

107

Karen Tolchin:	That's so true! I would *totally* put him in art therapy. I'm "all up in his grill," as they say.
Kyle Mercer:	There's a huge consequence for him to share anything with you, right? If he tells you the truth, something is going to happen that he may or may not like. It's way too charged an atmosphere to tell you anything.
Karen Tolchin:	Well, I've been *trying* to defuse it. I've been pulling away when he talks about death and destruction. I'll say, "I don't want to have conversations about blood and poop. I *do* want to have conversations about other things, *nice* things."
Kyle Mercer:	It's still manipulative. He's still triggering you.
Karen Tolchin:	Wait, now I'm confused. I can't say, "That doesn't interest me?" I'm trying to be authentic, and the authentic, God's honest truth is that I don't want to engage in that kind of conversation.
Kyle Mercer:	Get over it. You're not really listening to what he's saying. Charlie's saying, "Quit asking me about what my day was like."
	What you're trying to do is control him to give you the answers you want. "I don't want to have that conversation, I want to have *this* conversation." You want him to want to have a conversation about his day that he doesn't want to have.
Karen Tolchin:	But I don't think it's making him happy either, though. The death and dismemberment talk is all-day-every-day right now, and it doesn't seem to make him especially happy or peaceful. Like, nobody ever wins the war.
Kyle Mercer:	He's keeping this up because it gets traction with you. You got clean and untriggerable about the

whole "Fat Mama" stuff, so he's found another way to get that traction. If you have no traction and you just walk away and don't engage in it, don't react to it in any way, you just let it be, it will go away of its own accord when you don't give it any energy.

Karen Tolchin: But I thought saying, "If that's what you're going to talk about, I'm going to go in another room because that's not what I want to talk about. That's not something that interests me." I thought that was not giving it traction.

Kyle Mercer: No, because it still has traction with you, Karen. I can hear it in your voice.

Karen Tolchin: Okay, fine, I'll admit it—I really do hate this talk. It's the opposite of what I want. I want Charlie's mind and his life to be full of positive things, not gore.

Wait, I just heard myself there. The revision should be, "I want my *own* life to be full of positive things." Maybe since it isn't, I have no tolerance for what Charlie is reflecting back at me.

Kyle Mercer: That's right. Now, let me model a different way of talking with Charlie. Do some death and dismemberment talk with me.

Karen Tolchin: Okay. But actually, the very worst part of our conversations isn't even about that. It's when I walk away from that kind of talk, Charlie will often say, "How come you don't love me?" My choices are either "Stay and take the abuse, like a battered girlfriend" or "Abandon my child."

Kyle Mercer: Oh, I see what's going on here. Charlie's *totally* working you. He's got the fishhook in. He's pulling and pushing it. He's jerking you all over the place.

Let's do a little role-play around this. Let's have the conversation.

Karen Tolchin: Okay. You start. You're me.

Kyle Mercer: Okay. [A long pause ensues.]

Karen Tolchin: Wait, you're not going to say anything?

Kyle Mercer: Nope.

Karen Tolchin: That's so funny! I was waiting for you to start the conversation, but that's the whole point, isn't it? I really need to stop coming at him, is what you're saying.

Kyle Mercer: If I'm you, what do I need to talk about? I don't have anything to say.

Karen Tolchin: This is half the problem! At this point I don't think there's a single sentence I know how to mutter to Charlie that is not completely wrong from the **Stop Parenting** perspective. I feel as if I have just enough knowledge to know that I'm doing everything wrong, but not enough to do things right. It's like getting a new ski instructor after decades on the slopes. You were doing fine, but suddenly, you can't even seem to stay upright.

Kyle Mercer: If I'm you, I don't have anything to talk about with Charlie. What do I have to say unless I want to get into his space, right? I don't particularly want to be in his space right now.

Karen Tolchin: True enough. Okay. All right, I'll start the conversation as Charlie. Hi Mommy.

Kyle Mercer: Hi.

Karen Tolchin: Do you want to play?

110

Kyle Mercer:	I might. What were you thinking of?
Karen Tolchin:	I want to take this toy and I want to bounce it on your head.
Kyle Mercer:	No thanks.
Karen Tolchin:	How come you don't love me? How come you never want to play?
Kyle Mercer:	The games you're proposing don't sound fun to me.
Karen Tolchin:	They're so fun. I could cut your head off! That would be so fun. That would be so funny. Wait, how come you're not saying anything, Mommy?
Kyle Mercer:	I think I'm going to go cook some dinner.
Karen Tolchin:	Okay. So—Kyle—the only way to handle this situation is just to detach completely?
Kyle Mercer:	It's nonsensical. You just need to see his pain in it. It's just Charlie's pain. Nothing else, just his pain and his struggle. If you don't engage in his coping mechanism around it, eventually the pain and the struggle will come out.
	If you don't feed it, eventually it's going to wither and something else will come out. Your only job is not to feed it in any way. I can feel sad or compassionate that that's what he wants to engage in, but I just have no interest in that. I have no interest.
Karen Tolchin:	You mentioned his pain and his struggle. It's hard for me to consider Charlie being in pain and not do anything about it. Could he be struggling over stuff like being rejected by his friend Connor? Connor has pulled back from him for some reason, and sometimes he tells me about

111

	it. Charlie will say, "Connor doesn't like me anymore." If he said that to you, what would you say?
Kyle Mercer:	Okay. The first thing is, I really want to emphasize how we got to this point. If you don't ask him, he will still probably share that information just because he wants to.
Karen Tolchin:	Got it.
Kyle Mercer:	Why don't we model that conversation? You be Charlie being authentic, and I'll be you.
Karen Tolchin:	As a side note, before we start, I'm sure this is the first of many moments like this—he'll gain friends and lose them, and suffer. So, more generally speaking, I'd love to know how best to help our kids through social rejection and cruelty, which can be such a hallmark of childhood.

Use Inquiry rather than parenting to help children find their own truth about the world.

Kyle Mercer:	Okay, great. Let's do some Inquiry around this. You be Charlie.
Karen Tolchin:	I hate Connor.
Kyle Mercer:	What do you hate about him?
Karen Tolchin:	Connor is so mean. Connor stopped being my friend.
Kyle Mercer:	Do you have any sense why that was?

Karen Tolchin:	He is horrible and I should cut his head off. He wants to cut my head off.
Kyle Mercer:	How does it feel to you when he isn't your friend?
Karen Tolchin:	I don't care. I hate him.
Kyle Mercer:	It sounds like you do care about it, or you have some feelings about it. Hating is kind of like caring.
Karen Tolchin:	He didn't come to my birthday party.
Kyle Mercer:	How do you feel about that?
Karen Tolchin:	I think he didn't come because he doesn't like me anymore.
Kyle Mercer:	That's the *thought* about it. How do you *feel* about it?
Karen Tolchin:	Sad.
Kyle Mercer:	Where do you feel the sadness in your body?
Karen Tolchin:	My nose.
Kyle Mercer:	Are you sure? Why don't you close your eyes and check?
Karen Tolchin:	In my heart.
Kyle Mercer:	In your heart? Yeah. What's it feel like in your heart?
Karen Tolchin:	Stone.
Kyle Mercer:	Like a stone in your heart?
Karen Tolchin:	Mm-hmm (affirmative).
Kyle Mercer:	Do you want to keep carrying that stone in your heart?
Karen Tolchin:	No, I want to throw it at Connor's head.
Kyle Mercer:	Do you think that will work?

Karen Tolchin:	I think he could fall down and there would be blood and it would be so funny.
Kyle Mercer:	That stone in your heart, you can let it go if you want to and I can show you how.
Karen Tolchin:	Okay.
Kyle Mercer:	Okay. If you imagine that stone in your heart, and that was all the sadness you felt about Connor not coming to your party, would you like to let that go?
Karen Tolchin:	Yes.
Kyle Mercer:	Okay. Would you like to try what I do?
Karen Tolchin:	Okay.
Kyle Mercer:	Okay. First, do you want to let the sadness go?
Karen Tolchin:	Yes.
Kyle Mercer:	Now—Karen—if he said no, you'd have to respect that. If he *did* say no, I'd say, "Let me know if you ever do want to let it go." And then I would leave him alone.
Karen Tolchin:	Got it.
Kyle Mercer:	But let's say that he says "yes."
Karen Tolchin:	Okay, yes.
Kyle Mercer:	Where do you feel the sadness in your body?
Karen Tolchin:	In my heart.
Kyle Mercer:	Okay, great. Now, imagine you take all that pain. Wrap it around your heart like a steel band. Tell me when you've got it all there.
Karen Tolchin:	It's all there.

Kyle Mercer:	Then take the deepest breath you ever took into your heart and burst that band and let it go. Let all that sadness drain out of you.
Karen Tolchin:	Whoosh…
Kyle Mercer:	Check and see if there's any left and take another breath, let is all out. What do you feel now?
Karen Tolchin:	Whoosh….
Kyle Mercer:	Great. What do you feel now?
Karen Tolchin:	Good.
Kyle Mercer:	Okay great. Karen, did you get the feeling of how I gave no traction at all to his stuff around cutting off heads and throwing rocks?
Karen Tolchin:	The war talk?
Kyle Mercer:	Yeah. It's like it wasn't even there. I came back to what was real.
Karen Tolchin:	Okay.
Kyle Mercer:	Could you feel what it was like to give it no traction?
Karen Tolchin:	I could, absolutely.
Kyle Mercer:	It's like it's not even there. I just ignore it. I just go on with the conversation like it's a real conversation.
Karen Tolchin:	It's become such a huge part of Charlie's presentation with me that I'm anticipating that if ignore it, he'll think I'm ignoring him. Then he's going to get very angry with me.
Kyle Mercer:	That's fine. Let him get angry. Let's take a look at what that would look like.
Karen Tolchin:	Okay.

115

Kyle Mercer:	You be him being angry about it.
Karen Tolchin:	How come you don't listen to me? You don't love me. Nobody loves me.
Kyle Mercer:	What would you like me to hear from you?
Karen Tolchin:	I'm trying to tell you all these things!
Kyle Mercer:	What kind of things?
Karen Tolchin:	About heads being chopped off and poop and stuff.
Kyle Mercer:	I'm not interested in those things anymore.
Karen Tolchin:	No fair! How come you hate me?
Kyle Mercer:	I don't feel that that's true for me.
Karen Tolchin:	It is true.
Kyle Mercer:	I see. What would you like to do about all that?
Karen Tolchin:	Honestly, I'm not sure what Charlie would say. I need to try this with him.
Kyle Mercer:	Hmm. Trying it is different than doing it or being it, right?
Karen Tolchin:	Okay, I need to do this—and be this.
Kyle Mercer:	Again, it can't be a turtle.
Karen Tolchin:	[laughing] Kyle, you've already shown me that it's turtles all the way down!
Kyle Mercer:	I understand. Just let me clarify one thing: You're engaging in this Inquiry with Charlie so that *you* can be at peace, right?
Karen Tolchin:	Correct.
Kyle Mercer:	Good. As long as you're doing it to mold him, to make him a decent person, all that garbage, you've lost the thread again, right?

Karen Tolchin:	Right. It's what you call "that little parenting thing" again—the urge to shape and mold someone into a decent person. "Now, now, Charlie. Talking about chopping off heads is bad!"
Kyle Mercer:	You're just doing this because the truth is, you're not interested in that kind of talk. He's just another human being that lives in your household.

Your child is imprinting for who you are, not what you say.

	Imagine if Charlie were your roommate. Would you be interested in that kind of talk? No way. To engage, you would expect a certain level of decency. To be interesting, we have to generate interest in another person. Charlie might be losing his friends because he's relating to them the same way he relates to you.
Karen Tolchin:	Right. I've had my share of bad roommates, and I've changed situations as fast as possible to escape them. So, I'm enabling Charlie to continue behaving in a way that's going to harm him socially?
Kyle Mercer:	You allowing Charlie to continue doing what he's doing means that he's not going to learn how to relate to people right. You don't fix that by *teaching* it, you fix it by *being* it—by being in an authentic relationship to your child.
	You make Charlie so special and so important, you don't treat him like a person.

117

Karen Tolchin:	Holy cow. Something just clicked for me around all of this. I've been looking for answers to the questions, "Where do I teach, how do I teach, how do I guide?" I want him to have good friendships and I want him to have positive experiences. You're saying that by simply being in an authentic relationship with him, that's the entire lesson. If I stick around for all this war talk, then Charlie will think that's normal. Then, when friends like Connor back away from it, he won't understand why.
Kyle Mercer:	That's right. It's a lesson way beyond anything else because you're being an evolved human being. Your child is going to turn out to be just like you no matter what you say. All the lessons in the world make no difference. He's imprinting for who you are, not what you say. He's not even old enough to understand what you're saying.
Karen Tolchin:	Wow, that feels true. Terrifyingly true.
Kyle Mercer:	You are hypnotically imprinting your beingness on Charlie.
Karen Tolchin:	That terrifies me. The stakes seem too high. I don't want to imprint my uncertainty in the world; I want to imprint my groundedness.
Kyle Mercer:	In a way, Charlie is mirroring you back to you. This is great for you. His talk about death and dying, he's mirroring your lack of authenticity in the relationship. He's being equally as inauthentic as you are. Do you get that?
Karen Tolchin:	Sort of. How do you mean that?
Kyle Mercer:	Your niceness—your tendency to act nice even when you don't feel it, to be sweet and

cheerful—it's actually polarizing. He's just taking the other side of the argument. He's being Mr. Nasty. You get nicer and he gets nastier. I think you're being equally inauthentic as he is.

Karen Tolchin: Well, I'm trying so hard to get away from negativity...

Kyle Mercer: ... that you're practically forcing him to take the negative stance. He's balancing you out, mirroring your inauthentic positivity.

Karen Tolchin: Right.

Kyle Mercer: On some level, he's just saying, "This is how inauthentic you're being." He's like, "I'm going to *show* you how inauthentic you're being."

Karen Tolchin: I'll confess, I'm not acting with a lot of authenticity these days, Kyle. I have a house full of in-laws and family, and I'm trying to make everyone happy...

Kyle Mercer: All right, this highlights another cultural misconception: that anybody else in the world is responsible for our feelings. It's so wrong. We have to change our relationship to this terrible idea.

Last night, I was hanging out with a woman, and she said, "I hurt your feelings," or, "I made you frustrated." I said, "You've got to stop saying that. If I'm frustrated, it's about *me*, not about *you*." After all, I don't want to be responsible for *your* feelings; your feelings are about *you*. As far as I'm concerned, everybody else's behavior is neutral when I'm at my highest state.

Did you notice when I was teaching the Mountain Experience that I was totally neutral about everybody's feelings? I'm caring but I'm totally neutral.

Karen Tolchin: That was such a remarkable thing to witness. We get so little neutrality these days. To see you stand so calmly in the middle of so much emotion was really something.

Kyle Mercer: The idea that anyone is responsible for somebody else's feelings is ridiculous. That's a big part of family entanglement. People say, "You don't want to come to Christmas this year. You're hurting my feelings."

Karen Tolchin: That's so true! Christmas seemed to be a real quagmire for a lot of folks at the Mountain Experience. I heard multiple people talking about it as a hot button issue. They were saying things like, "I feel an obligation to do such and such, but it isn't bringing me joy. It's just that I don't want to hurt anyone's feelings."

Kyle Mercer: Exactly. I go, "What? How could I possibly hurt your feelings? They're yours. They're over *there*. If you're really interested in why I don't want to come to Christmas, we could talk about that." They might say, "Okay, why don't you want to come to Christmas?" I would say, "Well, the kind of Christmas *I'd* like to have would be like this: We try to be safe for each other. I just want to be in a place that feels like there's a lot of safety and caring and love. I just don't experience that at Christmas." They could ask, "Are we making you feel bad?" I would say, "No, it's fine. You guys can do Christmas any way you want. I'm just not interested." Right?

Here's the main point: This is not for you to fix. "We want you here at Christmas." If your family says that, you could say, "Okay, well then, this is the kind of Christmas I'd like to have. If you'd like to engage in a conversation about how we could have that kind of Christmas, then I might be interested."

The question is, why would you go if you didn't want to?

Karen Tolchin: Well, *my* answer would be, "So I don't damage any relationships by *not* going." But clearly, that doesn't really work for people.

Kyle Mercer: That's right. It doesn't really work for anyone.

Karen Tolchin: It's a little bit like, "You do you and I'll do me." If you really want to be happy.

Kyle Mercer: Happy is an interesting word. The more fundamental aspect would be total acceptance of what's true. Then, the being happy is not giddy or joyful. It's just content with what is.

Karen Tolchin: Another thing I noticed during the Mountain Experience is that we all have the full range of emotions in us—both the beautiful emotions and the horrible emotions.

Everyone is responsible for his or her own well-being.

Kyle Mercer: That's a bit of a misunderstanding right there: beautiful versus horrible emotions. That has to do with our societal prejudice against emotion.

121

We need all of our emotions, just in the same way you wouldn't want to lose any one of your other senses, right? Like, "Oh, I've got this sense of touch, but some things that I touch, I don't like what they feel like, like fire." I don't want to get rid of the sense of touch, but I recognize that if I'm touching something like fire... The bad sense helps me know that I wouldn't like to touch that.

Karen Tolchin: So there's a range of feelings in us. They're neither good nor bad, they're just varied.

Kyle Mercer: Negative emotions are just information about what's going on. The problem is, we get so prejudiced, we start generating our own emotions, rather than just using the natural ones that arrive. We start applying our emotional biases to our children, and now it's a mess. Consider the feeling of guilt, for instance, with our child. It's supposed to be a momentary sensation that lets us know that we behaved poorly in that moment, not a lifetime inheritance.

Guilt is like, if there's four pieces of bacon on the table, and four people, and you ate two of them, you feel guilty. "Oh, I shouldn't have done that, I ate more than my share," but you're not supposed to feel guilty for the rest of your life about it. You're just going to say, "Hey, I'm sorry, I ate more of the bacon than I should have. You can have them all tomorrow," or something. That's what guilt is supposed to do to us. "Oh, that was inappropriate." It's not supposed to be something that I then live in and bathe in. I'm branded a bad person, a greedy bacon-eater for the rest of my life. I'm going to have to atone for my sins, and be totally insecure with everybody who didn't get bacon, for the rest of my life? That's ridiculous!

Karen Tolchin: As an observer at the Mountain, it seemed to me that people had really been harmed by their parents' emotional lives. It was as if the excess emotion that parents had around parenting had become toxic. If everyone had just calmed down and been less either sycophantic and loving and gushing on one end of the spectrum, or neglectful, abusive, and hurtful on the other, we'd all be fine.

Kyle Mercer: Exactly. We create narcissistic children by making them so important. It's totally dysfunctional; they're not.

Karen Tolchin: Right, and at the same time, we neglect to make *ourselves* important.

Kyle Mercer: That's right. We give children this inflated idea of their own value and importance, rather than letting them discover it for themselves. It makes them totally insane.

We're making crazy people.

CONVERSATION #9:

Don't Come Home 'Til the Street Lights Come On

Lately, I've been thinking of how hard it is for me to keep up with my child. I had Charlie when I was almost thirty-nine, and now I get why people are supposed to get cracking at the whole parenting business in their early twenties, back when people have some stamina to spare. Despite having cystic fibrosis, Charlie seems to have enough energy most days to power an entire city. Most days, he rises at 6:00 a.m. and keeps going until 8:30 at night. He hasn't taken naps since he was two. I'm beginning to feel as if I should be training like a triathlete to keep up with him. Of course, it doesn't help that I'm still expending lots of pointless energy every day, fretting when I could be meditating, spreading myself thin when I could be prioritizing what really matters to me. I'm not sure how much of my fatigue comes from my age and how much comes from my choices. I might be too tired to figure it out.

For other parents in similar situations—because many of us are having children later in life, due to medical advances and a host of other factors—I broach the topic with Kyle. Our conversation ranges from parental guilt over not wanting to play all day with our kids to the ADD epidemic to transgender children to the decline of meaning-ful coming-of-age rituals in our culture. As ever, Kyle's perspective is unique and changes the way I see my own behavior as a parent.

Karen Tolchin: I'm having a devil of a time keeping up with my own kid. He hasn't napped in years, and I feel as if I'm perpetually disappointing him when I don't feel like playing with him all day long. I feel guilty for having caregivers step in, but I almost feel as if I'm renting their energy. Do you have any thoughts about this? Am I causing Charlie any harm by lagging behind?

Kyle Mercer: There's two aspects of this. Part of that wild energy is a function of the parenting environment.

Karen Tolchin: What about the parenting environment?

Kyle Mercer: Well, let me put it this way. I have a theory that much of the modern ADD and ADHD epidemic has to do with the parenting environment. We're stoking a fire. There are some kids that just have high energy levels. There are some who are wound up. Part of the great tragedy that started to change before I was born is that kids used to just get out of the house and play for hours and hours at a stretch. "Go away!" That's the right answer to that high energy. It's, "Go away, be back by dinnertime."

Karen Tolchin: That's true! Parents used to say, "Come home when the street lamps come on." I had that sort of freedom when I was an elementary schooler in the seventies. My parents never fretted about being interesting playmates for my brother and me. They were at work, but we had a neighborhood full of kids to play hide-and-seek with, or whatever.

Kyle Mercer: Exactly. When parents become their children's primary playmates and source of social interaction, kids want to run that high kid-energy with us. We should just be honest and say, "We're not interested."

125

"Get out and move!" That's what we should say. Instead, we coop them up and have them sit and play video games. Video games seem like the right answer because otherwise they act too wound up, but it isn't. Kids should go and do their own thing, ideally outdoors.

Karen Tolchin: I just can't imagine saying I'm not interested in playing with Charlie. "Want to play, Mommy?" "Nope, sorry, not interested." Wouldn't that scar his psyche for life?

Kyle Mercer: Being inauthentic is what causes damage.

Our children become a primary relationship where we've got them strapped to our hips and they're driving us crazy. They need to go out and exercise. Remember the study that showed that four hours of exercise can have the same effect as Ritalin? These kids really need to move their bodies.

Karen Tolchin: I can see that. There's a book called *Leave No Child Inside* by Richard Louv that talks about the cultural harm done by cooping kids up indoors. Apparently, we all think the world is less safe than it was in the seventies, especially regarding child abduction, but the statistics show the opposite is true. At the same time, childhood obesity has become a major threat to kids.

Having said that, you're not completely against the use of medications like Ritalin, are you?

Kyle Mercer: You'd think I would be, but because our culture is what it is, and schools tend to be the way they are, it makes it very difficult to have children just be free to run outdoors for hours at a time. If we are going to put children that are more active and high energy in our current schools, it creates a lot of suffering, not to have them be as free as they want to be. In some cases—just for their non-traumatization—I can see medications being okay for that, even though it's not ideal.

It'd be wonderful if we had school systems that honored children that naturally have a lot of energy. Children that naturally want a lot of activity, that naturally want to do things with their hands. Ultimately, instead of medicating all these children and shaming them into different behaviors, we need to create environments that will work *with* them.

Karen Tolchin: I believe that *most* kids would prefer to move around than to sit in a chair all day long. Most adults too, for that matter.

The Atlantic ran a great piece by Hanna Rosin in 2014 called "The Overprotected Kid." She describes a movement to restore independence and an element of danger via things like "adventure playgrounds." They're huge areas where kids can make their own forts, set things on fire, make tire swings, etc., with just one or two adults way on the periphery in case a fire goes out of control or something like that. (By the way, I'd love to become the sort of mom who could drop her kid off at one of those places for the day, and then not feel compelled to hide behind a tree and make sure he stays safe.)

I think a lot of parents in my generation believe that if we're not willing or able to meet our

127

children on that primary playmate level, all day every day, we're failing. I know I feel that way.

Kyle Mercer:
Exactly. We've overplayed with and engaged with our kids.

In yoga, my Indian teacher talks about children in the womb experiencing the bliss state, the deep meditation state of bliss and oneness. It's imprinted there for us to come back to. He says that little babies sometimes go into it. In our culture, what we do is they're glazed and spaced out because they're in this bliss space with God, and we want to stimulate them back and bring them back. My teacher says, "No, don't do that! That's terrible." If you were sitting there in meditation and were all blissed out and I said, "Come play with me! Wake up. Let's play cards," You'd be like, "What the heck are you doing?!"

We over-play with, over-read to, over-attend to our children, and it creates that narcissistic engagement with parents as if we're some kind of toy. We're not. If you look at other cultures, the parents are doing their own thing.

Look, kids can be a nuisance. We foist play on them instead of waiting for them to come and ask for it. It's like, "Go play." It's wonderful.

Karen Tolchin:
What if your child asks you to play?

Kyle Mercer:
If they come and ask for our participation, they could say, "Mom, I want to play." You could say, "What should we play?" They could say, "Let's play a board game." Okay. We sit down and play a board game and they start cheating. You'd say, "I'm not interested anymore." They'd say, "No, play with me." You'd say, "I only want to play if we

follow the rules." "Why?" "It's just not fun for me this way."

Now we start to teach them and engage them in an authentic relationship. Then the parents are like, "When you play you have to follow the rules." It's as simple as if you wait until they come to you and want to engage, now you have some power and engagement.

If you're always needy for your child's engagement, they have the power in the engagement, and you don't get to teach them anything. They're teaching you. They're saying, "If you want to play with me, you have to let *me* cheat, but *you* can't cheat." This is backwards.

Karen Tolchin: That makes so much sense! My parents noticed that I always let Charlie change the rules and win when we play games; by contrast, they don't. What a difference one generation can make!

Kyle Mercer: Listen, I have total compassion for moms. You had this child in your womb. You're attached with an umbilical cord. You shared that child in your womb and you created an attachment. That attachment is natural. It's a natural attachment that's supposed to protect the baby and all those things.

Karen Tolchin: I read that we actually swap cells with our children when we're pregnant. Male cells have been found in their mothers' tissues after women die, in women who haven't been pregnant for decades. Something to do with "cellular chimerism," which I don't really understand, but it confirms the depth of our connection. It's neither one-way nor temporary.

129

Kyle Mercer:	The bond is very strong. The trouble is, you have to get out of your own neediness. Your neediness comes from your unmet childhood needs. They make you want to relive your childhood through your child, so you get dysfunctional.
	If you can imagine a very noble mother that's not demeaning her adulthood and self-respect and that stuff to be in a relationship with her child, she would have a nobility of bearing. She would be loving and caring and compassionate and not controlling.
	I don't know if you can get the feeling of that.

We have no authentic coming-of-age rituals anymore.

Karen Tolchin:	Very much so. It's a beautiful image.
Kyle Mercer:	That nobility also means you have to recognize your attachment to that child is in interference with that child and it needs to be pared down. It needs to be gradually eliminated and handed off as the child's able to hand it off. Our timeline for that is very amiss. It's totally backwards.
Karen Tolchin:	Right. Jewish mothers in particular have a running joke about our sons: "What do you mean I'm holding on too tight? Whether he's ready to fly or not, I'll let him go by the time he's thirty."
Kyle Mercer:	Exactly. Boys in particular, at a certain age are supposed to be removed from the maternal sphere. Ideally, the men in our culture are supposed to

come in and cut the umbilical cord and take the boys into the world of men. Take them out of the world of women. Mostly in our culture, the boys are getting abandoned by their fathers and left in the world of women. As a result, they never learn how to be men.

Karen Tolchin: Also, they get very angry.

Kyle Mercer: The women get angry, too. It drives women crazy that they're with little boys instead of men in their own adult relationships. That's a vestige of the fact that the men aren't showing up for the boys. We don't have men in our culture.

Karen Tolchin: The little boys stuck in the world of women, I think, are pretty angry.

Kyle Mercer: Yes, or else they never develop those qualities of masculinity and become less masculine in the world.

Karen Tolchin: At some point I think it would be great if you could explain how you define masculinity and femininity. Parenting around masculinity and femininity is especially important right now, and gender identity. As our cultural awareness increases about things like transgender issues, this is very much in parents' minds right now. How do I support my child's gender identity, gender development...

Kyle Mercer: It all comes back to just supporting your child.

Let them have their own experience and be a safe place for them to come back to.

Just love them the way they are. That's the thing. This is just another influence and we're so crazy. I mean, we are insane about sex on many levels. One is we hide it, and the other level is we're so interested in it. That gets passed on. You're never going to be able to protect your children from the influence of what's going on in culture. Whether you like it or not, it's out there.

The very best thing to do is let them have their own experience, be a safe place for them to come back to when they go out and have experiences in the world. Use Inquiry, rather than parenting, to help them find their own truth about it.

Karen Tolchin: I think that can be especially difficult. That can be an area that's especially hard for parents because, as you say, we are all kind of psycho about sex to begin with. We're full of shame.

Kyle Mercer: What I'm proposing with **Stop Parenting** takes a tremendous amount of courage and a tremendous amount of focus. You need to muster the courage to let go of control. You have to have the courage to be willing to just be open and hear what your children say rather than trying to manage it.

Karen Tolchin: We've talked a little bit in our coaching calls about rites of passage. I wonder if you could say a little about coming-of-age rituals and their importance?

Kyle Mercer: At one time, that's what the Bar Mitzvah meant. It's a modern attempt at a rite of passage, but nobody starts treating that child like an adult after their Bat Mitzvah.

Karen Tolchin: That's true. No thirteen-year-old is going to be treated like an adult in our culture.

Kyle Mercer: On a global basis, there is no rite of passage.

What it's *supposed* to mean is that your whole childhood is finished. That's part of what we do at the Mountain Experience, we let go of all the emotional pain we carried. If you were to have a complete rite of passage, we'd do the Mountain Experience and the Freedom Experience and the Matrix Experience.

Muster the courage to let go of control. Hear what your child says and quit trying to manage him.

Your childhood is finished. You made it here. Clean the slate. You get a fresh start. You get to be whoever you're going to be, and nobody is going to bring up who you used to be. You get to recreate your life any way you want.

133

Karen Tolchin: Could you talk a little about that story I once heard you tell, the one about the monsters in the village swooping down to kidnap the boys?

Kyle Mercer: Sure! I think this ritual is from Indonesia…

What happens is, every few years, the men dress up as monsters and they come into the village in the middle of the night to grab the boys. The women are in on it, but they act just as if real monsters are stealing their children. They moan and they wail and they say, "Don't take my child! I can't live without him."

There's this tension and this breaking that solidifies that metaphorical cutting of the umbilical cord. Then it no longer exists, and the boys are taken away for six months.

Oftentimes, our parents just teach us about our weaknesses. In this sort of rite of passage—and there are similar ones in Native American culture—you would go off and you'd be taught about your strength. There'd be a ritual around pain where you were taught your strength to endure pain, also maybe endurance, maybe courage. You'd come back with your strength and a clear sense of your identity, and who you were that came from the Great Spirit or from a vision quest. You'd have a spirit animal or a direction or be clear. In that process you'd know what your qualities were in the world.

You'd come back knowing yourself in a new way. We're supposed to have these at different stages in our life over and over again, these rites of passage.

Karen Tolchin:	Wow, there really is nothing like that in our culture. Everyone seems to remember what you were like at five and continue to throw it back at you forever. I believe that's why going home for Christmas feels so unsafe to so many people: because they've left home to redefine themselves as adults, and Christmas—or Hanukah, Thanksgiving, whatever—just throws them back in the soup.
Kyle Mercer:	All the rites of passage used to be like that. People wouldn't even talk about what you were like as a child because you had become an adult. Your parents weren't your parents anymore. The sky became your father and the earth became your mother. Your parents were no longer your parents. There are other aspects to that. That's just one nuance. I'm using that nuance to make a point. You were new and fresh in the world.
Karen Tolchin:	I just sat through our college's most recent graduation ceremony. The graduation seems like a ritual that was invented to do something similar, like a pale, last vestige of what you're describing.
Kyle Mercer:	It's one of the only effective rites of passage we have left. If I go to school for psychology, right before graduation I'm not a psychologist, and right after, I am.
Karen Tolchin:	There's a profound change, a clear line of demarcation from before to after.
Kyle Mercer:	The ceremony makes the truth. Ceremony is very important. We have it at the Mountain Experience. The ceremony for Creating Sanctuary makes it much more true than talking about the idea of it.

Karen Tolchin:	Absolutely. I was surprised by the power of the Sanctuary exercise. That was such a rare gift you gave us. At the same time, the rareness of it seemed wrong to me.
Kyle Mercer:	It's bizarre, I agree.
Karen Tolchin:	I really liked the way you had us do things physically to demonstrate our consent at various points. "If you agree to create a safe space for each other, to create sanctuary, take a step forward." You had us communicate by moving our bodies.
Kyle Mercer:	You're making that external commitment to other people.
Karen Tolchin:	Making it visible.
Kyle Mercer:	Ceremony is a way human beings make abstractions real. Like marriage. The wedding ritual is a good example.

Spanx Are Great Under Tight Dresses, but That's About All

I t occurs to me that Kyle and I have yet to tackle one of the biggest taboos of contemporary parenting: Corporal punishment. Since we've talked so much about the value of not interfering with our children and their development and their growth, I think I know what Kyle believes. After all, it seems pretty obvious and clear that there is so much disrespect involved in raising your hand against a child, it would be totally antithetical to the whole spirit of **Stop Parenting**. But Kyle always surprises me. What if my belief that spanking is bad turns out to be one of those cultural canards? I decide to ask him about it point blank.

Karen Tolchin:	Brace yourself, Kyle. I have a tough one for you today.
Kyle Mercer:	Great! Go ahead, hit me.
Karen Tolchin:	Funny you should use that expression. What I want to know is this: What is your position on spanking children?
Kyle Mercer:	Well, using violence to try to change somebody is wrong on so many levels. I mean, the violence part, especially when it goes along with shaming somebody, or making them wrong about who

they are, or enforcing that there's something intrinsically wrong with them—it's terrible.

When I work with people that have been punished physically, and it goes along with shame, it just puts it at a whole other level of emotional pain that they carry. Its being reinforced physically is a huge amplification of the impact.

Now, on the other hand, when we talk about setting boundaries for ourselves to not be interfered with, there is an appropriate use of force to get somebody to stop doing something that's harming me.

So, shaming with violence is terrible. Using appropriate force to stop somebody from doing something that's harming me, or to interfere with the harm—the dramatic harm—of somebody else, would be appropriate.

Karen Tolchin: I can understand that.

Kyle Mercer: For instance, I have used forceful language to stop Henry from doing something that was violating me.

Karen Tolchin: Have you raised your voice?

Kyle Mercer: Yes, I've raised my voice, but again, that's not ideal. I've only used that to set boundaries for myself that weren't being respected, as opposed to trying to teach him to be different than he is. That's the most important distinction.

In certain cases I think it's appropriate to use physical means to set boundaries.

Karen Tolchin: How do you mean?

Kyle Mercer:	When Henry was a baby, he had this thing where he would become upset if he was flailing around, and swaddling him would calm him right away. Some babies do really well with being swaddled, which is tied up tight and bundled, right?
Karen Tolchin:	Sure, most babies love being swaddled. It's the first thing nurses teach you after delivery. It's very comforting.
Kyle Mercer:	There are children that have … because they haven't received enough attention, they really need some containment to feel safe. This is a more difficult, complex subject. That's a different issue than being controlling; it's recognizing that children at different stages of development just need to know that somebody's there. There are certain behaviors that are there just to try to get attention. It's usually a response to abandonment at some level. Now, there's some kids that are just wild and at certain times just need to feel the presence of containment.
Karen Tolchin:	You talked a little bit, too, recently about how teenagers sometimes need a different kind of container than children. Is this related to that?
Kyle Mercer:	Yes, it is. It just really makes a big difference at what stage in the child's development you start or you stop parenting. The earlier the better, because in my experience, the not-parenting tends to correct these things.
	It's important to recognize that **Stop Parenting** is different from abandonment. In **Stop Parenting**, the idea is to be very present with our children without controlling them. They do want our

139

	attention and presence. They want to feel us there.
Karen Tolchin:	I'm so glad you made this distinction. I made that mistake myself when you first said the words **"Stop Parenting"** to me. I equated it with abandoning my child. Now, I see that **Stop Parenting** requires even more presence, authentic presence. A lot of focus, too, and self-discipline.
Kyle Mercer:	Oftentimes, I will have a parent say, "My kids are just dragging at my legs all the time. They want my attention. They're always screaming for it. I'm trying to get things done." I say, "Just having present time is necessary for children."

There was some study that 95 percent of parent-children communication is corrective and only 5 percent is interactive. Really, it needs to be the other way around. It can be as simple as a child that is really trying to get our attention, just sit down with them and give them your full attention until they're ready to do something else. It may only take five minutes until their tank's full of attention, and then they're perfectly good to go off on their own. A lot of times children are just looking for our presence. You could also just sit down with some art supplies and instead of telling them what to do, watch what they do. Participate in what they're doing without directing or guiding.

| Karen Tolchin: | What you're describing sounds exactly like a program we learned about last year in Vermont. It's called "Parent Child Interaction Therapy" (PCIT). |
| Kyle Mercer: | [laughing] Also known as just paying attention to your child. |

140

Karen Tolchin:	True! But it's also a formal behavioral therapy program that really works. So many kids act out because they are starved for genuine interaction.
Kyle Mercer:	I think it's funny to call it therapy. It's like humanly interacting with your child as a human being is a therapy. That's funny.
Karen Tolchin:	Well, it's funny to think how little we just organically do this in our culture. It's like, how often do we offer each other the sort of sanctuary you created at the Mountain Experience? So simple, so profound, and yet so rare. Maybe we need to formalize these things because we've grown so far in the wrong direction.
	I literally had to be taught how to pay real attention to my child. I had to sit down with someone and be taught that five minutes where I'm not multitasking, where I am 100 percent present with my child, where I'm not guiding, but just being with him, was enough to restore a lot of balance to our household. I had no idea how directive I was being. If we were sitting down with LEGOs, I would say, "Oh, do you want to build a house? Let's do it this way so it won't topple over." Or if Charlie wanted to draw a face, "Don't forget to put the head on top of the body." Imagine if Picasso's mom had been that directive.
Kyle Mercer:	Exactly.
Karen Tolchin:	What if the house wants to wobble, and the nose looks better next to the belly button? Who put me in charge, anyway? Just being together in a non-directive way can make all kinds of problems evaporate because that's what children are

141

really hungry for and not getting because we're all so amped up and we're all so ... Our phones are going off every two minutes and we're over-scheduling ourselves and over-scheduling our kids.

I loved PCIT, but my parents were so skeptical. They were very much like, "Oh, just spank him" when he was acting out. Tom and I said, "Parents don't do that anymore." They were like, "Oh, for God's sakes. You're spoiling him." Then, a year later, just last month, they shared this article from *Washingtonian* magazine with me. Apparently, the hottest pediatrician in the entire city–his practice is full–is teaching parents how to do this. All kinds of behaviors, all the crazy, over-active, violent behaviors, all this kind of stuff is just completely dissipating.

Kyle Mercer: That's great.

Karen Tolchin: It really is. There's this groundswell of people who are hungry for a different way of relating to their kids. There's a wonderful blog called "Free-Range Kids," a book called *Bringing up Bébé: The French Way of Being*, which is really very much in line with what you're talking about. You don't make your child the center of the universe in an unhealthy way. That child should be integrated into your universe.

Kyle Mercer: *Oui.*

Karen Tolchin: The other thing that I've noticed is that, while most of my parenting books are opposed to spanking for many of the reasons you've mentioned–ineffective, damaging, etc.–they still have a strong flavor of "spare the rod, spoil the child." They all say, "Get in there, even when it's hard... Manage their homework, insist on this and that, get involved at every level, even if they want you to get out of their business... Be active in your parenting." I used to agree.

You've helped me see that it doesn't much matter if we're no longer beating children anymore to accomplish our goals if the goals remain the same. The tactics have just gone underground, in a Foucauldian sort of way. If we're still interfering via our language and our posture, we're still causing harm.

Kyle Mercer: That's right. I think of it this way: We're indoctrinating children into the cult of family. It's the same kind of brainwashing techniques that a cult would use.

We're indoctrinating children into the cult of family. It's the same kind of brainwashing techniques that a cult would use.

As a teacher, I'm deprogramming people from the cult of family. A lot of my work is that the belief systems and the punishments and all those things that have come in need to be cleared out. To some degree, we all need to be deprogrammed from the cult of family. You can tell by the extent of the deprogramming you need just how functional your family was.

Karen Tolchin: Here's another hard question. If you have a child who seems to be headed down a path of drug abuse or self-harm like suicide, you might look at this philosophy and say, "Well, if I follow this advice and **Stop Parenting**, my child could die."

Kyle Mercer: I get that and there's a few aspects to that. One aspect is that, to a large extent, it means that we've already parented.

Karen Tolchin: Do you mean, we've already done some harm? Are you equating the verb "to parent" with the verb "to harm"? That's pretty radical.

Kyle Mercer: What we should be doing is encouraging children to explore the world and have their accidents and their own mistakes and their own learning, and then have a safe place to come back to. But that's not what most parents do.

We might think that parenting's safe, but it's really not. Parenting is a form of criticism.

Karen Tolchin: "Parenting is a form of criticism"? Well, that explains a lot. No wonder so many people rebel against their parents.

Kyle Mercer: That's right. Parenting isn't safe, it's an implied judgment that there's something wrong with you, that you don't have what you need.

Kyle Mercer: Now, a child that is really, truly a threat to themselves and/or others and at risk, I would not advocate zero action. Sometimes, I actually recommend that parents send their children into programs that help the children have direct life experience. There are a lot of great programs

144

Eric

out there where they take teenagers and give them direct experience with nature or other environments where they have to face their own behavior in a similar way they might have to face it out here in the world.

Traditional parenting isn't safe. It's an implied judgment that there's something wrong with you, that you have to be whipped into shape.

This isn't politically correct, but a lot of times these children are very entitled children that have very narcissistic viewpoints. They've been abandoned by their parents because of work or their parents' own interests or whatever. For whatever reason, the parents just have not been that interested in being present in their kids' lives.

Karen Tolchin: So, these parents didn't **Stop Parenting**, they just abandoned their kids, right? Having some sort of a nature boot camp experience can be a corrective to that?

Kyle Mercer: Yes. Allowing nature to give natural consequences is a really powerful way of maturing someone.

Around the beginning of the teenage years, our children are supposed to have the opportunity to come into their own, to go out and have

145

difficult experiences and transcend them and let go of their parents and become an adult and take responsibility for themselves. This is just another key element that we're not having. We have grown adults that are still acting like children in our culture.

Karen Tolchin: In the case of, say, someone who does seem to be set on a path of immediate self-harm, or harming others, would you advocate intervention?

Kyle Mercer: Yes, I would.

Taking Stock of the Losses Involved in Stop Parenting

As I reread the transcripts of my calls with Kyle, many things occur to me, the cumulative effect being that I'm feeling pretty disheartened. I've devoted my life to education, and have generally been a quick study—Chemistry notwithstanding—but I'm beginning to feel like the class dunce. I'm having the hardest time acquiring this knowledge, probably because it's the sort of thing that goes way beyond the brain. This isn't ordinary book learning, it's about radical spiritual growth. I used to dabble in spiritual growth the way I would pick up and drop a new hobby, in a half-curious, dilettantish way. Now I see that if I don't make progress and fast, my kid may pay a steep price his whole life. I also have an inkling that this work would be equally urgent even if Charlie didn't exist. It's not like quilting or tennis: it's the most meaningful engagement of my life.

I'm getting the **Stop Parenting** gestalt on a surface level, but I'm not truly inhabiting it the way Kyle recommends. I desperately want to evolve and embody that calm, peaceful, enlightened mother that Kyle has described for me on multiple occasions: "She would have a nobility of bearing. She would be loving and caring and compassionate and not controlling." Kyle said he once saw an older woman kneeling in her garden, bathed in sunlight, completely whole and at peace in her solitude, and he got that feeling from her. I want to be this sort of ideal mom. An enlightened mom wouldn't run herself ragged. She wouldn't act nice and happy and positive if she didn't genuinely feel all of those things. She wouldn't arrange her life so that she felt frustrated so much

147

of the time. She wouldn't live and die over every conversation with her young son. She wouldn't need him to be happy and healthy and fulfilled and connected to her the way I seem to need Charlie to be. She would take care of her own needs and model a way of being in the world that could inspire her child to create a great life for himself. I'm acutely aware of the extra baggage I'm yoking to Charlie, yet I can't seem to stop stuffing the packs. I'm growing horribly self-conscious in my own home.

*In a private coaching call, I confess to Kyle that I feel like a **Stop Parenting** failure. If publish and go on a book tour, what on earth could I offer to other parents who are struggling? "I'm pretty sure this is the best way to parent. I hope you have better luck following the program than I have." I've been thinking and being one way in the world for four and a half decades. Am I too old, or too hardened into my twisted shape, to change? If so, what will that mean for Charlie? What will that mean for me?*

Karen Tolchin:	Reading back over all of our transcripts, I feel a little bit depressed. In conversation after conversation, I'm beginning to see that it's lots of different versions of me saying the same thing: "I really want to interfere. I really want to intervene. I really want to keep parenting in an action-verb sort of way."
Kyle Mercer:	Mm-hmm (affirmative).
Karen Tolchin:	In conversation after conversation, your part is mainly to say to me, in lots of different ways, "**Stop parenting**. Knock it off, do less, say less, just be."
Kyle Mercer:	That's right.
Karen Tolchin:	I have *writ large* the proof of just how hard-headed I am, and how very difficult it is for me

to give up my old ways. I must be afraid of losing something. Could we talk a little bit about the losses around **Stop Parenting**?

Kyle Mercer: That's a really good question. Here's what I think makes it so hard for everyone, not just you.

When I'm parenting, and I'm engaged in that process, I feel like I'm building somebody into a human being. That means that I'm anticipating being responsible for the wins that my child has in life. It's like I get a second lease on life, in a way. All the things I didn't do, all the things that I did wrong. It's like I'm projecting my life into theirs.

For you, there could even be other factors. Your relationship with your brother, with your parents, there's all sorts of things. Aspects of dysfunction and loss that you're trying to correct. You're making this huge personal investment in there with the hope that it will pay dividends and save you and fix you, in a way, even if it's externalized.

It's this huge project. There's a lot of hope invested in that.

Karen Tolchin: Yes, there is.

Kyle Mercer: There's a lot of hope it will be revealed that "I parented well," or a lot of hope that that person will have a life that redeems me in some way. It's so misplaced.

With **Stop Parenting**, we're giving up the hope of it being said that we're a great parent. We're giving up the possibility of people acknowledging that, of our children saying, "You did such a great job." At the same time, I recognize it. It's like, "Wow, I've done such a good job not parenting that I don't get to take any credit for how wonderful Henry is, and his achievements." There's a loss in that. They're all his.

Karen Tolchin: Henry did it all by himself?

Kyle Mercer: That's the truth. They're all his own wins and losses. I get complimented a lot around how great he turned out. Most of that doesn't land. The one thing I say is, all I did was just stay out of his way as much as possible. Some people say, "Wow, that's not easy," or give me a compliment on that and say, "That's really wonderful that you were able to do that." It's just important not to inflate into that.

Now, can I ask you a question?

Karen Tolchin: Of course.

Kyle Mercer: You can always edit this out.

Karen Tolchin: Okay, but I'll try not to. I'm hoping someone who reads this will benefit from my struggle.

Kyle Mercer: If your stubbornness was a function of guilt or shame, what would be the energy behind it? Stubbornness is "I'm taking a stand, I'm going to be a good parent or I'm going to get Charlie well, or I'm going to make him safe, or I'm going to have him have a good life." Where is the stubbornness in your parenting coming from?

Karen Tolchin: I think it's fear and hope.

Kyle Mercer: Okay. What's the fear?

Karen Tolchin: Fear that if I don't do something correctly, then my child will suffer.

Kyle Mercer: What will that mean?

Karen Tolchin:	It would mean he wouldn't have as meaningful a life, as happy of a life, he wouldn't become the person he wants to become, he wouldn't be able to manifest his life the way he wants to manifest it.

I'm much more conscious now of interfering, and I'm definitely doing it less, whenever I recognize it. I think some of this has gotten through to me. I'm not laboring under the same illusions. I don't think I'm supposed to provide all of the scaffolding for my child's life anymore. But now I think, "What if I still interfere too much and mess him up?"

To sum up, I'm afraid that I'll either do or not do something, and Charlie will pay a steep price. |
Kyle Mercer:	Let's say somebody was laboring to save you from your suffering. What would that feel like?
Karen Tolchin:	Intrusive.
Kyle Mercer:	Intrusive? What else?
Karen Tolchin:	They would have to assume that I'm suffering, so potentially misunderstood.
Kyle Mercer:	Misunderstood, sure. Also being rescued implies that you're weak.
Karen Tolchin:	Right.
Kyle Mercer:	Even this idea that suffering can be avoided in life is quite an illusion. We all suffer in life.
Karen Tolchin:	Hearing you say that makes me think of my family. In our home, showing concern was a primary way of showing love. When my parents showed concern for me when I was a child—going to school with me to confront a bad teacher, for

instance—I really felt their love. They were so tapped out with my brother's health most of the time, those occasions really took a lot of extra effort.

Kyle Mercer: I see. Isn't that interesting? Concern is an interesting word because it can be used two ways. There's two implications, right?

Karen Tolchin: How do you mean?

Kyle Mercer: Concerned, sometimes we just use it to mean being attentive. We can also use it to mean worry.

Karen Tolchin: Right.

Kyle Mercer: For you, worry is being attentive, is loving.

We all get informed what love is. I worked with one person for whom hate was love. He grew up in a household where the only way that people showed that they cared was through their hate. That is care, by the way. If somebody doesn't care, they don't have any feeling towards you. To hate you means that they have a tremendous amount of care. It's negative care but it's still a tremendous amount of connection. The only way they really knew how to love, because they didn't have any other example, was around hating.

Co-dependency, in our culture, is the classic form of love that we receive and then pass along. At best, that's simple exchange. It's, "I'll do for you if you'll do for me. I'll worry about you if you worry about me. I'll worry about you if you behave." We don't want to get stuck in exchange when we could relate to each other in much higher ways, like collaboration and contribution.

Karen Tolchin:	Right. I don't want my relationship with my son to be transactional. I *definitely* don't want to communicate to him that he's weak and in need of my rescuing him. I want him to grow up knowing that he's strong.
Kyle Mercer:	The only way that he can grow up to learn that he is strong is by him dealing with his own suffering. When you address his suffering, he learns he's weak. When he addresses his own suffering he knows he's strong.
Karen Tolchin:	So, when I swoop down and fix everything, then he gets the message that he can't take care of himself?
Kyle Mercer:	He never learns to.
	A simple example, when I teach people to teach their children letting go, is the steel-bands-around-the-heart meditation. That teaches children that they have the strength to let go.
	When you try to fix it, feed it, coddle it, all that kind of stuff, that's just putting a fake bandage on it. That's coping. When I feel bad, I'm going to get nurtured. Now I should feel bad a lot so I can get nurtured a lot.
	How about we let people let it go, and then get nurtured when they're happy or feeling good? It's not that we shouldn't be present for them when they're feeling bad, but it's much better to teach them their own strengths than their own weaknesses.
Karen Tolchin:	I'd *much* rather teach Charlie his strength.
Kyle Mercer:	And teaching it to him is just uncovering it.
Karen Tolchin:	That's true. It's already in him.

Kyle Mercer:	Little babies, if they're crying because you're not there or because their diaper's messy or whatever, as soon as you change it, they're better. They let it go. They don't keep harping on about it.
Karen Tolchin:	They don't go, "It was so horrible earlier when I was wet!"
Kyle Mercer:	Yes. Then we start *unteaching* them the skill of letting go that they were born with. It's insanity.
Karen Tolchin:	This is something I really need to work on. If I can see a quick and easy way of taking away suffering, I'm a little bit notorious for doing that. "Mama can fix that for you!"
Kyle Mercer:	Well, because you have a resistant and oppositional child, when you're trying to reduce his suffering, what is he going to try to do?
Karen Tolchin:	Suffer more.
Kyle Mercer:	Yes.
Karen Tolchin:	Super. That's the very last thing I want.
Kyle Mercer:	You said you had fears and hope. The fear was around your child's suffering. What's the hope that you're attached to?
Karen Tolchin:	The hope is that he's going to grow up knowing that he's strong and grounded, and he's going to manifest the life that he wants to be living.
Kyle Mercer:	Right. That can only come from his own inner agency. As long as you take the agency for his life, he'll never learn that.
Karen Tolchin:	Okay. What are some of the ways that you take away your child's agency with your hopes for your child? Would it be something like my

saying, "I hope Charlie wants to do a semester at sea someday!" Because I love the sea, and the salt air might keep him healthy.

Kyle Mercer: Those are *your* hopes, not his. Find out what *his* hopes are.

Karen Tolchin: Right. Okay. Once again, the right answer is to use Inquiry.

Kyle Mercer: That's right. Now, when we start working with children in their teens, there's kind of another layer of teaching that comes in that's not parenting. There are times later on when it is appropriate to address, or bring our awareness or observation to that teenager.

Karen Tolchin: Can you give me an example of that?

Kyle Mercer: I don't want to go too far into this. It might be a whole other book, but for teens, sometimes it's important to reflect to them what they're doing.

One time I asked Henry a question. I'd gotten him an iPhone and he was definitely getting attached to it. He was playing games with it all the time. I went in and I said to him, "Henry, how do you feel when you're playing those games?" He looked up and he said, "I never thought about it." He checked in and he came in a little while later and he said, "I don't feel that great when I'm playing these games. I feel kind of anxious or stressed." Then he said, "I've got an idea. I'm going to get a bunch of kids together and I'm going to film them while they're playing a game. Then I'm going to take them skiing and I'm going to film their faces while they're skiing. I'm going to see how many times they smile and what makes them smile the most. I'm quite sure it's skiing."

Karen Tolchin:

It's so great that it came to him naturally! If you had come down like a hammer and said, "This is bad for you, I'm limiting your access to the phone," as so many parents do out of fear, he never would have acquired that knowledge for himself. You would have inadvertently made the iPhone seem better and better to him.

Kyle Mercer:

"I don't really smile when I'm playing a video game." Such great firsthand knowledge!

Karen Tolchin:

So, it's appropriate then to be guiding a little bit in the teen years?

Kyle Mercer:

It is, but it's a little different... There's a little bit of confrontation around it. Instead of just letting the world parent him. If we were in tighter communities, that wouldn't be the parent's role, but there is some container that we create for teenagers that's important.

Karen Tolchin:

Your iPhone anecdote reminds me that so much has been written lately about the rise of the "screenager" population. I wonder if you could just say something generally about the fact that when we all go into restaurants now with our kids, one of the first things we do is plug our children in.

Kyle Mercer:

Yeah, well, with Henry, one of the great things about the Waldorf education is it really discouraged electronics, so until Henry was about ten or eleven, he had very little exposure to electronics and I think that served him very well. I think, in all things, balance. I think when children are younger, it is better to keep them away from that, and we, as a culture, we haven't really been exposed to these things for long enough to know what effects they have on us. At the same time, we don't want to be neurotic about it, and it's really hard to tell whether this interfacing with computers may become the way of the future, and because we're older, we judge it. Again, it's part of the world, and I think that, as in all things, it's good to have balance around it.

My approach to all these things is ... I mean, food, all the kinds of ways of restricting the children or saying no, I want to eliminate as many of them as possible. I don't keep unhealthy food around the house so I never had to correct unhealthy food. For the young child, we took everything out of the house that we had to say "no" to, and I was happy to live in a house that only had kid food, so I didn't have to correct. We just didn't have electronics and we didn't have a TV. We didn't have those things in our lives, and I chose to live my life without them. That was the kind of parent I wanted to be, and I found that it was beneficial for Henry.

Karen Tolchin: That makes so much sense. I forget that I'm the adult. If I'm living in a chaotic space, I have the power to change it.

Kyle Mercer: That's right. Another word about food: I think we make kids neurotic about it. We gave Henry the things that he wanted to eat. We didn't try to make him have a broad diet and all that kind of stuff. We just kind of trusted him to know what was good for him.

157

Karen Tolchin: Right, but on the other hand, you didn't have a house full of Twinkies, right?

Kyle Mercer: Exactly. If he was out, he could get those things and we wouldn't say "no" but we just didn't live that kind of lifestyle. I think there's a lot of hypocrisy out there. Your children will be like you.

Karen Tolchin: I realize our conversations are really skewed to toddlers and younger children because those are the pressing issues in my own household. I'm sure there's going to be room later for tackling the world of the older child and the adult child.

On the other hand, there's so much in our manuscript about how the best way to be a parent is just to parent yourself. The basic principles here, I'd be shocked if they didn't carry through from parenting an infant to parenting an adult child. Or unparenting.

Kyle Mercer: The future conversations build on this one. It's levels of development, and this is not a layer that is left behind, but is part of the developmental process. I have a whole seminar, the Matrix Experience, where I take everybody through their levels of development, and we recognize what's handed off at different levels. There's actually a number of stages of development that are really profound. First there's the womb, and then

It's critical that we do our own spiritual work as parents. We need to parent our children from a place of wholeness.

there's the next two years which is the external womb, where the child is still dependent. That's where there isn't any parenting to be done. It's just nurture.

When they get a little more capable around 2 and this stage from 2 to 9, 10, 11, even 12, this is the part where they are now individuating. Then the next stage is the teenage stage. Level 3 contribution is the stage at which we bond with our mind, our mental abilities, our capacity in the world. That next stage is really important during those school years, the teenage years, where we're really allowed to see that we're creative, that we have good ideas, that we have a capacity to invent. Inquiry is really powerful there as we allow our children to come into their contribution. If we keep foisting our ideas and our beliefs on them at that stage, it starts to repress them and say there's something wrong with their creativity, with the way they think, with the way their mind operates. This is where we get people not really feeling as if they have much to contribute or offer in the world. Our school system doesn't support that.

Then, the next stage is adulthood. Adulthood, this early adulthood, is where I become fully responsible for meeting all of my needs. Where I learn that I can meet all my needs and that I am the source for myself. If I don't get that … How I've experienced these matrices in the previous stages is how I own them for myself. If I've been heavily parented and then I come in to try to be an adult and still feel I need parenting—I'm still looking for all this parenting outside. Where do I look? I look to media. I look to popular culture. I'm not looking within me, I'm checking outside me. We want to set up this foundation so that they have access. This is why peer pressure works: because I'm still looking for a parent outside the parent.

Karen Tolchin: There are so many great examples in literature and film of that, looking for the parent outside the household, in appropriate and inappropriate ways. Every coming-of-age narrative has this theme.

Kyle Mercer: Most adults in our culture don't ever fully fill out adulthood. If I go into the next stage, which is maturity, with these voids, and now I have children. All of the voids, all the places I haven't filled within myself are going to be transferred into my children and I'm going to project in that they need parenting, that they need whatever it is, that they're not okay. It just goes on and on.

Karen Tolchin: Turtles all the way down!

Kyle Mercer: That's why it's so critical that we do our own spiritual work as parents. We need to parent our children from a place of wholeness. We're already dented and banged, we need to acknowledge this. We can't be perfect, but we can bite the bullet and behave as if we are. Right? We can do our work and continue to do our work, but at least stop thinking that we have any parenting to do, or that we're a better judge of what they need than they are. We're already dented and twisted from our experience.

Karen Tolchin: Right. Coming at it from a place of real respect, that's where I see so many parents failing, particularly with older children.

Kyle Mercer: That's right.

Karen Tolchin: With teenagers, there's so often just a total lack of respect on both sides. Parents say, "I don't understand you and your music and your haircut and your friends. I have an image of how you should be and who you should be hanging out with and how you should be spending your time, and I don't want to hear about what you are choosing for yourself." Kids reflect the disrespect back.

Kyle Mercer: That's right. In our house, it's very different. Henry got angry at me the other day because he's ready to be on his own. He said, "You don't give me anything to resist!" Which was actually a lovely compliment.

Karen Tolchin: That's pretty extraordinary. "I'm rebelling against the lack of any reason to rebel!" I'd love it if you would repeat what you told me about how when you were first coaching, before you'd become a parent yourself, you tried to talk to parents and help them, but you didn't have any credibility.

Kyle Mercer: I remember distinctly because I used to run trips that were rites of passage on this river. It was a

161

five-day river trip and we went through all the traditional rites of passage aspects. It was for adults
and they'd also bring their children. Everybody
in our culture needs a rite of passage because
we didn't get one. Most of us are still operating
with broken voids and need to take full responsibility for our experience. We tend to want to
externalize it and blame other people and those
kind of things.

Karen Tolchin: The river trips sound amazing.

Kyle Mercer: We were on the river and somebody was ask-
                   ing about his teenage children. This was before
                   Henry. I started to tell him to **Stop Parenting** and
                   he said, "You'll see how terrible it is when you get
                   there." I knew. Even then I knew. There's nothing
                   I can do with that because they've already made
                   up their minds that parenting is suffering. I just
                   refused to believe that parenting was suffering. I
                   refused to believe that we have to parent to have
                   our kids be okay. It's insanity. That happened to
                   me every year. After I had Henry, people would
                   say, "How is it with your two-year-old? They're in
                   their terrible twos, right?" I said, "No, it's great."
                   They'd say, "Wait until he's four." Then when he
                   was four, people would say, "Wait until he's six."
                   Then it was like, "Wait until he's eleven. Wait until
                   he's a teenager."

Karen Tolchin: "Wait until he's a teenager. Then you'll really be
                   sorry!"

Kyle Mercer: Exactly! Well, I'm still waiting. And I've never
                   been sorry.

CONVERSATION #12

Controlling for Happiness, or When the Dolphins Mutiny

I'm beginning to integrate Kyle's philosophy. I've started to recognize when other parents are being snared in traditional parenting traps. Another mom at Charlie's school confided that she was bracing for the moment when her lovely, compliant ten-year-old daughter became a teenager, and all hell broke loose. "Everyone keeps telling me to batten down the hatches," she said. "Teenaged girls are the worst." I shared Kyle's river guiding anecdote, about all the parents who warned him about a rebellion from Henry that never came. I said, "I bet if you just hold onto the idea that those people don't know you, and they don't know your child, and there's no Armageddon coming, instead of bracing for it, you'll be fine. Just let go of that silly idea and I'll bet it will never happen."

She looked at me in wonder. It was like, "What? You mean I have a choice? I don't have to accept the disaster narrative that every parent on the planet is giving me about the teenage years?"

In this conversation, I share my success, and then move into a conversation about where I'm still struggling. In particular, I learn that I've been approaching Sunday family boating with the wrong attitude. As usual, Kyle wastes no time setting me straight.

Karen Tolchin: When you teach something, it helps solidify the knowledge, and I really felt that by helping this fellow mom not fear her daughter's gruesome transformation to come—like a zombie apocalypse—I was stepping out of the traditional parenting model.

163

Kyle Mercer:	That's great! We still want to honor the truth that teenage girls can be oppositional, but the real question is, "Do we need to have a problem with the opposition?" If you don't have a problem with the opposition or you're not trying to fix it, then it can be happy and joyful and you can even play with the opposition, right?
Karen Tolchin:	I would love to say, "Right," but I have no idea what it would look like to "play with the opposition." This could be really helpful with me with Charlie, since he loves to say "Black" when I say "White."
Kyle Mercer:	Well, a classic one is when the teenager says, "I'm so embarrassed." You say, "What are you embarrassed about?" "Mom, you're such a dork." "Yeah? There's that. How am I a dork? Tell me more, I'm really curious." "Mom, you're such a dummy." "Tell me more about that, I really am curious about it. How else am I a dork?"
Karen Tolchin:	It just takes all the heat right out of it, if you inquire into it.
Kyle Mercer:	That's right. I was just talking about this with somebody who has an adult child who's always raging at them. They're always trying to correct the raging. I said, "They're just trying to get it said! Give them a chance to get it said, for God's sake." They're just begging to be heard. You won't let them. They're going to keep having to say it until you hear them.
Karen Tolchin:	Just stop trying to control. Let your child be heard.

Kyle Mercer:	There could be a lot in it for you to hear there, if you're open to it. If you're closed to it, they're going to keep screaming it at you more and more, louder and louder, until you hear it. Everybody who keeps going off and saying stuff, they keep getting louder because you haven't heard them yet. That's where Inquiry comes in. All you have to do is, you drop into Inquiry and you start saying, "What bothers you about that? What's upsetting about that? What did you want me to hear about that?" If you don't have to resist it, if you don't have to correct it to prove that you're a good parent to them and everybody else, then you can stop and actually listen to them.
	That's the whole key to **Stop Parenting**.
Karen Tolchin:	You know, it hit me after our last conversation with Tom, where it became clear that a lot of the work I need to be doing both with Tom and with Charlie is letting go of this idea that I can make our family experiences fun. It's just going to be what it's going to be. I can't will a morning on the boat into a joyful, happy outing.
Kyle Mercer:	That's because you can't make anybody else happy. People can only decide to be happy.
Karen Tolchin:	I think that I have not truly, fundamentally grasped that. I think, "If I set the stage for happiness, and just give everyone all the tools for happiness, it will happen. If I put us on a boat and it's a sunny day with beautiful blue water, and there are dolphins leaping around us, we can't help but have a nice time." I mean, who doesn't love dolphins?
Kyle Mercer:	Right. Wrong, obviously.

Karen Tolchin: Totally wrong. Completely wrong. If someone's going to enter that situation with a foul temper, there aren't enough leaping dolphins in the ocean to make that a happy outing. That's an area where I think I've been really stubborn and I think a lot of other parents have been really stubborn right along with me. It's the classic Mom dinner scene: "I set this beautiful table, and you sit down and tell me that you hate green beans.

Even trying to control for happiness is wrong. You're allowed to have your own happiness, but to foist it on others is an intrusion.

And your sister comes and tells me she'd rather eat with her friends. And your father would rather be watching his football game on TV. Well, screw all of you!"

Kyle Mercer: "I'm doing it right."

Karen Tolchin: That's my anthem! "I'm doing everything right. Why isn't this working?"

Kyle Mercer: "Why don't you all understand?"

Karen Tolchin: Yes, it's like, "I don't get why you're not playing your parts correctly."

Kyle Mercer: Right, exactly.

166

Karen Tolchin:	"You're not reading your script the way I've written it." That's what's really wrong. It's controlling. It's trying to control people.
Kyle Mercer:	Yes. Even trying to control people for happiness is wrong.
Karen Tolchin:	Oh boy, that's huge for me. "Trying to control for happiness is wrong." That's so hard for me, personally.
Kyle Mercer:	You're not alone.
Karen Tolchin:	A few hours after our last failed outing on the boat, Tom and I watched a movie together. It was *Wild*, with Reese Witherspoon.
Kyle Mercer:	I'm aware of it but I haven't seen it. It was actually filmed here in Ashland.
Karen Tolchin:	That makes sense, since the author lives in Portland, Oregon. She's from Minnesota, and her name is Cheryl Strayed. It's a wonderful memoir and a very good film. So anyway, I watched it with this horrible boat ride fresh in my mind. The narrative is mainly about a young woman trying to get over the death of her mother. The pain and her grief, it's so intense. She calls her mom the love of her life. The grief is so intense for this young woman that she sabotages her own marriage, she has multiple affairs, she starts doing heroin. Just a lot of really dangerous, terrible stuff, all to numb herself. To try to escape feeling what she was feeling.
	Eventually, she decides to hike the Pacific Crest Trail as a way of coming back to herself. A huge part of that return to self for her is letting herself

	grieve. There's no pole-vaulting over that grief, she just has to go through it.
Kyle Mercer:	That's true.
Karen Tolchin:	The thing that I noticed this time that I didn't notice before, and I think it's because I was still mad about the boat ride, is about the mother. Reese Witherspoon plays the young woman who lost her mom, and Laura Dern plays her mother.
	I watched all the flashback scenes with Laura Dern. She's picked a horrible guy, he's abusive, he's beating her up, the kids are watching. There's a lot of chaos and violence in the house. When she finally leaves their dad and they go and they create a life for themselves, just the three of them, you see the mother trying really hard to create this happy, serene, positive, family setting. It works to a point. She's always smiling. She's always saying, "How much do I love you? Is it this much? Is it THIS much?"
Kyle Mercer:	This sounds familiar.
Karen Tolchin:	I know, very. She's this loving, like, "I just want to make everything okay for my children" type of mother. As soon as Reese Witherspoon's character gets older, she turns on her mother and she's so critical of her. Her mother is singing and dancing in the kitchen, and Reese just lets her have it in this horrible, snarky way. She says, "What the heck do you have to be singing and dancing about? We don't have two pennies to rub together. You married a terrible guy. Why on earth should *you* be happy? Why should you be dancing? Why should you be acting like this?" It

was a real rage that she turned on her mother who was militantly insisting on being cheerful.

Kyle Mercer: Exactly: It sounds as if the daughter is raging at the mother's militant cheerfulness, because it's not real. We're all yearning for what's real.

Karen Tolchin: Well, the answer that Laura Dern gives is, "I'm not going to regret that marriage because it got me you and your brother." She's not going to sit around in mourning just because she doesn't have a Maserati, or whatever.

Kyle Mercer: That's fine but it's a platitude. It's like the daughter saying, "You haven't felt it, you haven't experienced it. You're in denial and you're covering it up with a coping mechanism of artificial happiness."

Karen Tolchin: Oh. So that's what she's reacting against, the fake cheer?

Kyle Mercer: That's right. It's perfect for you because you do the same thing.

Karen Tolchin: Ugh, I *absolutely* do the same thing. What's funny is that just hearing your reaction, I'm learning a little bit more about it.

By the time the movie ended, I was really steamed. I said to Tom, "I see exactly how it is. Mothers are these incredibly sweet people who are killing themselves to make a nice cheerful home, and fun boat rides for everyone, but everyone around them is trying to poop all over that. Well, you'll all be sorry. The second we're gone, everybody is *crushed*." I was half-joking, half-serious. Not my finest moment.

169

Kyle Mercer:	But don't you see? That's the message: Go now. Let everybody appreciate you rather than foisting it on them.
Karen Tolchin:	Right. It's only on your own that you're able to locate your own authentic experience of happiness. It's not watching your mother dancing around the kitchen. Right?
Kyle Mercer:	Yes. You're allowed to have your own happiness, there's no question. But to foist it on others is an intrusion.
Karen Tolchin:	Right. An area where I'm still not clear is how to have my own happy life no matter what's going on. I think this might be something other parents won't readily understand, either.
Kyle Mercer:	It's simple. Give to yourself what you're trying to give to Charlie.
Karen Tolchin:	Can you say that one more time? Because it feels super important.
Kyle Mercer:	Give to yourself what you're trying to give to Charlie.
Karen Tolchin:	That really gets to the heart of the matter, doesn't it?
Kyle Mercer:	That's the end of the hypocrisy of parenting. You're really just ultimately trying to give it to yourself. All the things you want your child to improve, to be like, to do, to understand, to get— give it all to yourself.

Give to yourself what you're trying to give to your children.

Karen Tolchin: Okay, except now I don't know what to do on Sundays. I'm not trying to be stubborn.

Kyle Mercer: Do you want to go on a boat ride?

Karen Tolchin: I do, I love being on the water.

Kyle Mercer: Then give it to yourself.

Karen Tolchin: Tom and Charlie can go if they want to?

Kyle Mercer: Sure. Listen, if you want to go on a boat ride, you're actually the parent and children are dependent, so you can also make Charlie go, but you can't make him be happy. It's okay to make him go for *you*, just don't make him go for *him*. That's the hypocrisy.

Let's have the truth. It's the same as the school conversation. "Why are you going to school today? Because I need somewhere to put you while I'm taking care of myself." Be honest.

Karen Tolchin: Right.

Kyle Mercer: Instead of, "I'm doing it for you." That's the greatest evil, that I'm doing it for your own good. It's dishonest. "I'm doing it for my *own* good." Now we're talking. Now we've got the truth.

Karen Tolchin: Right. It's so hard to know what's good for your child, except for the most basic things. Obviously putting a hand on the stove is not good for your child. Eating nothing but Skittles is not good.

Kyle Mercer: That's not exactly true. Hand on the burner, yes we want to have them avoid major injuries, partly because it's such a nuisance to us. But the more we allow them the learning, the less parenting we have to do.

171

Every time we decide to intervene, we do some damage to the relationship. No matter what it is. If the kid's running towards the street, a busy street, you grab onto their arm and jerk them back. They're like, "Ouch!" You've done a little damage to the relationship. The trade off is worth it because they didn't die, but you've done a little damage to the relationship. We really want to put it in perspective. Of course major

End the hypocrisy of parenting. Stop thinking you're a better judge of what your children need than they are.

injury is not ideal, but major injuries have resulted in some amazing breakthroughs and awareness and these kinds of things. Who knows, what is Charlie supposed to learn from CF? That's some course on something.

Karen Tolchin: Right. It's quite an education, CF.

Kyle Mercer: That's a course on something. He gets to have his own learning from that. *You* get to have your learning about having a child with CF.

Karen Tolchin: Right. This idea of trying to rewrite history through our children, either an unhappy childhood, by rewriting our own—as seeing our own childhood as happy—or, we didn't succeed in a way we think we should have succeeded, so

	trying to push our children to succeed. These are all terrible intrusions.
Kyle Mercer:	Absolutely. Just getting honest. Even with Charlie it seems like "I'm feeding you for your own good," or "putting you on the Vest therapy machine for your own good." It's for *your* good as his mother. "Sorry, I really don't care if you don't like how I'm doing this because this is what I need to do so I can feel okay about myself." That's honest.
Karen Tolchin:	That's a pretty cold bucket of water, right there. I think the biggest thing that comes across re-reading our manuscript is how almost everything you can do or say as a parent is problematic. The less you do from the position of parenting, and the more you do and say from the position of, "I am a human being talking to another human being," the better.
Kyle Mercer:	The prevailing idea in modern parenting is, "I can do better than nature." Think about the arrogance of it.
Karen Tolchin:	Speaking of doing better than nature, there's been a lot in the news about vaccines—parents who are unwilling to vaccinate their kids because of fears about the medication harming them, and then diseases that were almost eradicated making a resurgence. Can you say something about how we make these choices as parents, and as a culture?

Every time we decide to intervene, we do some damage to the relationship.

Kyle Mercer: I'll just say the briefest thing. It's fine to express your style in the world. It's fine to teach your religion to your child. I mean, all of this stuff is fine. They get a choice when they have their right of passage to choose any religion that they want, to choose whether to vaccinate their children or not. Just be clear: It's not about your child, it's about you. It's about your expression, the same way, you wouldn't adjust the décor of your house to try to get it right for your child. You're just going to decorate the house the right way for you.

Karen Tolchin: A lot of people are saying, this is a public safety concern. People are expressing their personal beliefs in a way that's now jeopardizing the public health.

Kyle Mercer: That's why we live in a country that has freedom of belief.

Karen Tolchin: Right. Even if it ends up bringing back diphtheria.

Kyle Mercer: That's right.

Karen Tolchin: That's a hard pill to swallow for someone who likes to have at least the illusion of control. Someone who looks an awful lot like me. Through our entire manuscript, I really want to find out at the end of the day that it's actually okay to be parenting with all my might, and it's actually great to be intervening at every turn.

174

I keep trying to get around everything that you're saying and you keep leading me back and being like, "No, here you go again. No, there's no loophole here. You're not going to find it." That's why I started this call saying I just felt so thickheaded.

Kyle Mercer: Let it be what it is. Your fear is about letting it be what it is.

You're constantly having to fight with what it is rather than just saying, "I wonder what it is," and keep track and find out.

Karen Tolchin: Right. Do some Inquiry. It's the same thing you identified that I was doing at the Mountain, which is "struggle with life."

Kyle Mercer: Right. We all do it. I've got my struggles with life too. I get frustrated and all that kind of stuff. It's life trying to tell us to quit struggling. Every time we struggle, life's saying, "How about not struggling with that?" You're going to have pain or frustration or hurt, as long as you struggle with it. Life's just trying to patiently keep on showing you how you resist life. It knows that life just is. It just is. It's unfolding how it is. We have so little control and so little input. Life knows that happiness comes from surrendering to it.

Karen Tolchin: Right. Surrendering is key.

Kyle Mercer: In a way, life compassionately creates the pain to let us know when we *haven't* surrendered. Otherwise, we'd never get it.

Karen Tolchin: Okay. Maybe this is the crux of what I'm having so much trouble with. I have this feeling that surrender is weakness. Surrender is failure. Surrender is

	going down with the ship instead of fighting to keep it afloat.
Kyle Mercer:	Right.
Karen Tolchin:	Every single association I have with surrender is negative. When I got married, a coworker gave me a book called *The Surrendered Wife*. I think books are pretty sacred but I tossed it in a garbage can as quickly as I could.
Kyle Mercer:	It's a cultural thing, certainly, that we're supposed to go down fighting.
	A different metaphor you can use for this is a river.
	If you're floating in a river, and the water represents the flow of your life, what does it look like if you refuse to surrender to the river?
Karen Tolchin:	So trying to stop flowing?
Kyle Mercer:	Yeah, or trying to swim upstream, right?
Karen Tolchin:	Right.
Kyle Mercer:	How well does that work?
Karen Tolchin:	Not very.
Kyle Mercer:	I don't know if you've ever been in a river before, but how about swimming downstream?
Karen Tolchin:	Going downstream is awesome. It's great.
Kyle Mercer:	Well, you can *float* downstream effortlessly, but if you start *swimming* there, I assume you're going to get tired pretty soon, right?
Karen Tolchin:	Right.
Kyle Mercer:	The river is not going fast enough. Things aren't going quick enough. You're going to exhaust yourself. In a white water river, the instruction is

	to put your feet downhill so you can fend off any boulders, keep your head up and relax and try to stay in the deep water. Then you're prepared for what's unfolding.
Karen Tolchin:	A lot of this, I'm not even sure this is part of my nature. I think it might be an inheritance.
Kyle Mercer:	You've just been taught to fight. You're fighting your husband, you're fighting your son. You're fighting yourself. You're in a perpetual struggle, fighting everybody everywhere.
Karen Tolchin:	That's not very smart of me, is it?
Kyle Mercer:	It might be smart but it's not useful. A lot of people would tell you it's smart to fight. It has been smart in a way. Whether it's smart or not, it's whether you want to have that experience or not.
Karen Tolchin:	I don't, certainly not with Charlie. I realize I've created all this resistance. Another thing in this transcript that's really come out very clearly is that the **Stop Parenting** method is far more likely to yield children, people, who have a connection with what's intrinsic for them. Their thoughts, their feelings, what they want in life.
Kyle Mercer:	They know themselves, yes.
Karen Tolchin:	They know themselves, versus people for whom everything has come from extrinsic pressure. Then just trying to untangle what's extrinsic and what's intrinsic. I think my entire life has been extrinsic. I think I was raised very extrinsically.
Kyle Mercer:	We all were.

Karen Tolchin:	I think I have a lot of confusion about what's actually intrinsic.
Kyle Mercer:	Confusion is because we don't know who we are. That's what we're all trying to get back to.

Parents are a huge hindrance to our educational process.

	That's the real gift in using Inquiry in parenting: that our children get to know who they are and what's true for them, and, more important, *we* get to know who *we* are. Maybe that knowledge is more important than them getting through AP Calculus or something.
Karen Tolchin:	Absolutely. I just went to a Parents' Forum at my son's school, and people were asking things like, "Why can't I look up my child's weekly grades online?" The head of the school said, "That doesn't serve your kid and that doesn't serve you. We check in with you guys eight times a year and that's probably too much. Your child really needs to take ownership and share with you, if that's
	appropriate, or not share it with you." He understood that helicopter parenting is a disaster. "Let's not make our kids crazy by being overly attentive and focused on their every move" was his message. Instead, "Let's help our kids figure out who they are, and what's important to them."
Kyle Mercer:	Yes, that's right.

178

Karen Tolchin:	I'm just very glad about that. I'm very glad that we can afford to send him to a school that isn't also forced into lock step for these standardized tests. It's so very important. I think it's a *Stop Parenting* kind of school—with lots of support for their individual exploration, and an appropriate amount of pushback for parents who have lost perspective.
Kyle Mercer:	Parents are a huge hindrance to our educational process.

Penguin Love, or From Entanglement to Engagement

I go to Charlie's kindergarten class to read a book to the children. He has an amazing teacher named Mrs. Gardino who makes me and every other parent want to be a child again, and be with her all day every day. She's invited all the parents to come and read, and I've brought "Rainbow Rob" by Roger Priddy—a book so beloved in our household that its spine has to be held together with blue painter's tape. Rob is an amiable penguin who happens to look up at a rainbow in the sky one day and grows instantly dissatisfied with his lot in life. He wonders why he's stuck with a black and white palette when there are so many fabulous colors to choose from. He decides to try on every other color. When he finally comes to the end of his journey, he realizes that being black and white is just fine. Rainbow Rob realizes that he doesn't have to look outside himself for happiness. In other words, it's an Inquiry Method book if ever there was one, and I'm all too happy to spread the gospel.

Charlie is so happy to see me, and so proud, that he comes running across the room and leaps into my arms saying, "Mommy's here! Mommy's here!" It's possible that I've never been so purely joyful myself when I bury my face in his neck. I say, "Charlie! I'm so happy to be here. I'm so happy to be able to read to you and your friends." Charlie leads me by the hand over to the reading carpet where, almost the moment we sit down, his mood plummets. He was so happy, but now... it's like tropical weather patterns. That fast. A dark cloud moved in out of nowhere. He had been thinking, "Oh, having Mommy at *school is cool. Reading one of my favorite books with my friends will be fun," that sort of thing.*

What happens is, all of his friends climb into my lap, touch the book, and start talking to me. I can see the little wheels in his brain turning. He starts thinking, "Wait a second. Hold on, pump the brakes. Nobody said anything to me about sharing. I have to share my mother and my favorite book? This is the worst day ever."

When I get to the end of the book, Mrs. Gardino says, "Charlie, I want to get a picture of you with your mom." He's sitting next to me. "Please smile. Smile for the camera," she says. He shakes his head and buries his face in my lap. She's such a lovely woman, and she says, "Oh, I get it. It's really hard to share Mommy, isn't it?" No shaming or scolding or anything like that. He nods.

When I try to leave, all hell breaks loose. Charlie says, "Don't go. Take me with you. I hate Kindergarten. I hate it here. I hate these other kids, and I hate it here." I don't know what to say. I try this: "Well, Charlie I know it was hard to share, but you get me alone every night. You get Rainbow Rob whenever you want at home, and you don't have to share either of us most of the time." Then, I hug him and I kiss him and pry him off my leg with the words, "Have a great day."

I know there would've been a better way for me to handle the moment, but I can't think what it might be.

*Kyle has said repeatedly that **Stop Parenting** does not mean child abandonment, but rather a deeper sort of engagement that does not interfere with the child's development. But on some level, it still feels like abandonment to me—like a severing of the bond we have. One of the pieces that I have not fully grasped is how to continue to love my child deeply without loving him in a dysfunctional way. Kyle has pointed out all the ways in which my love has been codependent. It's been an entanglement and it's been a burden for my child. I think we've done a lot of work to clean that up, but it's left me a little bit uncertain. How deeply are we allowed to love our children? Does all* *love come with some vestige of codependence? How do I trade entan-glement for engagement?*

I bring my concerns to Kyle.

Kyle Mercer:	Let's try some Inquiry around it.
Karen Tolchin:	Great.
Kyle Mercer:	What did Charlie say?
Karen Tolchin:	He said, "Don't go. I hate it here. I don't want to share my book. I don't want to share you. All I want is to be with you."
Kyle Mercer:	Okay. "What do you hate about it here?"
Karen Tolchin:	"All these other kids. They don't love me."
Kyle Mercer:	"Hmm, interesting. What else do you hate about it?"
Karen Tolchin:	"I don't like this stuff here. I like my toys at home better."
Kyle Mercer:	"Anything else?"
Karen Tolchin:	"My teacher's mean."
Kyle Mercer:	"What else?"
Karen Tolchin:	"I think that's it."
Kyle Mercer:	"Well, I really appreciate that you liked having me here."
Karen Tolchin:	"Well, you have to take me home with you."
Kyle Mercer:	"Well, I'm not going to, sweetie."
Karen Tolchin:	"Well, why not?"
Kyle Mercer:	"Well, it's your time to be at school, and it's my time to not be a mom."
Karen Tolchin:	"But you're always a mom. You're my mom. You should always be my mom."

182

Kyle Mercer:	"I guess in a way I am, but this is my time to take care of things I need to take care of."
Karen Tolchin:	"Well, now I hate you."
Kyle Mercer:	"Okay, I understand."
Karen Tolchin:	"Life is so unfair. I hate life."
Kyle Mercer:	"Hmm. What do you hate about life?"
Karen Tolchin:	"I just hate how hard it is."
Kyle Mercer:	"What's hard about it?"
Karen Tolchin:	"Everything."
Kyle Mercer:	"Can you give me an example?"
Karen Tolchin:	"Well, nobody gives me Skittles anymore."
Kyle Mercer:	"What else?"
Karen Tolchin:	"That's all I want to eat. Well, nobody loves me."
Kyle Mercer:	"You feel like nobody loves you?"
Karen Tolchin:	"Mm-hmm (affirmative)."
Kyle Mercer:	"Is that true?"
Karen Tolchin:	"I don't know."
Kyle Mercer:	"You might take a look at it."
Karen Tolchin:	"What do you mean?"
Kyle Mercer:	"How can you tell if somebody loves you or not?"
Karen Tolchin:	"If they buy me presents."
Kyle Mercer:	"Oh, I see."
Karen Tolchin:	"In fact, you haven't bought me a present in a long time. You must not love me anymore."
Kyle Mercer:	"Yeah, you know I realized for me that buying presents wasn't how I wanted to express my love anymore."

Karen Tolchin:	"But I love presents and I love candy and life is so unfair."
Kyle Mercer:	"All right, sweetie. Well, enjoy the rest of your day at school. I love you. How about a hug?"
Karen Tolchin:	Wow, see what's different here I think is that I'm still focused on trying to get an outcome. Trying to get a resolution. What I felt in your energy was just this very deep, calm presence.
Kyle Mercer:	Eventually, I got a little bored with the conversation, especially when it just started to become nonsense, you know?
Karen Tolchin:	Right, right.
Kyle Mercer:	Frankly, I'm not interested in hearing about Skittles.
Karen Tolchin:	This relating in an authentic way like being kind, just being patient, being loving, but also being real ... All of that came across.
Kyle Mercer:	There's no entanglement. I'm not tied to him being happy or not happy. It starts to teach him that it's a choice.
Karen Tolchin:	Yes, I think I'm still tied. I drove off and my phone rang and it was one of my best friends, Leslie. She said, "How are you?" I said, "I'm a bad mother. How are you?" I said, "I just abandoned my child who was sitting under a dark cloud in his kindergarten class hating life. I just drove off saying, 'Good luck with that.'"
Kyle Mercer:	It's perfect.
Karen Tolchin:	"Good luck with all that misery!" I said, "I'm a criminal and should probably be locked up."

Kyle Mercer:	That aspect of being a bad mother, that's that big thing that we have to really accept. That's where the freedom is, in totally accepting that.
Karen Tolchin:	There's so much freedom in embracing that. I think I'm definitely making strides in the right direction--

The idea of good or bad parents is an egoic identity. I'm not a good parent or a bad parent; I'm just a being who has a child.

Kyle Mercer:	It sounds like it.
Karen Tolchin:	--but I still definitely get tripped up. Honestly, there's a place in my heart that wants to go, "Finally! I know just how you feel. I only want to be with you, too. Let's go away together and let's just hug each other and have a whole bucket of Skittles." There's an old Jewish joke about the mother who says, "Oedipus, Schmedipus—as long as you love your mother." I know that kind of love is the toxic equivalent of Skittles, not nutritious for either of us, but there's still part of me that thrills to it. After so much conflict, too, just any expression of love and closeness… I want to join him in it, no matter the hour of the day.
Kyle Mercer:	When you say you want to do that, is that really true?

Karen Tolchin:	What's funny is that most nights when I'm reading to Charlie I have trouble keeping his attention and I have trouble getting him into his books.
Kyle Mercer:	If you're having trouble keeping his attention, stop reading the book.
Karen Tolchin:	Good idea. But it's funny. All of a sudden when other children showed up and were really excited about my reading and my book, it became, "Wait a second. That's mine." There was a place in me that just felt like, "Oh, good. I'm really glad that you're seeing that all of this has value. I'm sorry you're suffering, but I'm glad you appreciate me."
Kyle Mercer:	Well, that's opening up a whole other realm of parenting that we're talking about, then. It's your ego, right?
Karen Tolchin:	How so?
Kyle Mercer:	You're parenting for your ego, to give value. Give it up. There's no value to give. Again, that's just for you. To satisfy your ego. Your parental ego. It's to do things for him. Just get out of his way. He'll let you know what he needs if you pay attention again.

A lot of times your assertion interferes with your paying attention. You're so busy with your idea of what should be happening that you don't pay attention to the impact your behavior has.

Karen Tolchin:	I feel the truth in everything you're saying. What feels incomplete to me, or unfinished, or conflicted, is the love component of all of this.
Kyle Mercer:	Okay. What does love mean to you?

Karen Tolchin:	Oh, God. It means so many different things. I guess when I'm talking about the love of my child I'm talking about a profound, deep connection and a care for him. A caring for him.
Kyle Mercer:	What does that caring do?
Karen Tolchin:	You know I'm at a point right how where I'm really not sure which direction to turn with it. I don't know what it does. I'm afraid it's doing harm and that's why I'm asking the question.
Kyle Mercer:	We have a lot of misunderstandings about love. I think one of the basic ideas of love is just wanting the other person to be happy. One of the tests you can give is looking at whether or not the way that you're loving is creating more happiness in the person you're loving. If it's not, then it's not love.
Karen Tolchin:	Sometimes I mistrust the size of my emotions.
Kyle Mercer:	Yes, and you ought to because it is out of balance, the size of your emotion. We know that that's something other than love.
Karen Tolchin:	What is it if it's not love?
Kyle Mercer:	I think part of it is giving yourself away ... You're trying to love yourself through your child, which is not true love. Thich Nhat Hanh has a great book called, "True Love."

Here are the elements of true love. The first is *maitri*, which can be translated as "loving kindness" or benevolence. Kindness is not only the desire to make someone happy, to bring joy to the beloved person, it's the ability to bring joy and happiness to the person you love. He goes on about that. The second element of true love |

187

is compassion. This is not only the desire to ease the pain of another person but the ability to do so.

Karen Tolchin: I guess where I'm getting confused is how that's not rescuing. How is that not interference or intervention? I've become very, very mindful now of the ways in which I might be inadvertently trampling on Charlie.

Is the way you're loving creating more happiness in the person you're loving? If not, then it's not love.

Kyle Mercer: That's where, again, the development as a parent is to not only want these things for your child but to be effective at delivering them. Delivering the capacity to ease someone's pain is really teaching them how to ease their pain themselves rather than fixing it for them.

It's really becoming a fully embodied person. Because your love a lot of times can be gushy and overflowing and all that stuff, it comes across in the wrong way.

Karen Tolchin: I'm trying to love from more of a place of a deep groundedness. The image that you gave me that was so helpful is focusing on being on more of an even keel.

Kyle Mercer: Yes, and experiencing your love rather than expressing it.

Karen Tolchin: Well, now, what do you mean by that?

Kyle Mercer: My experience of loving Henry is occasionally I'll let him know that I love him but at appropriate times. The rest of the time I'm just experiencing it within myself.

Karen Tolchin: I'm trying to picture this. You're not speaking love, but you're emanating it?

Kyle Mercer: Well, not even emanating but just experiencing it. I'm experiencing it; my enjoyment at being in his presence. I think there's this sense of, "I think she doth protest too much," when you have to express it all the time.

Karen Tolchin: Ah, got it. In an early call, I was talking about how much I love Charlie, and you said, "How come none of your stories show you simply enjoying him?"

Kyle Mercer: That's exactly what I'm talking about.

Karen Tolchin: I hoped that that was because I was bringing you all the problems and none of the good stuff to help solve them, but it really did stop me in my tracks and make me think, "Well, yeah. How much *am* I enjoying my time with him?" It's grown a lot easier to do that now that I don't feel pressure all the time to be a "good mother." Now, I think about just being a person with another person.

Kyle Mercer: That's right. It's important to constrain that a little bit, really. To be a little understated about things. Part of **Stop Parenting** has this quality of understated presence.

     That's kind of Yoda-like, you know? [makes some Yoda sounds.]

189

Karen Tolchin:	Yes, well, I'm much less wise guru and much more Broadway musical in my personality, so this is a major challenge for me. I'm more "Auntie Mame." Skittles for everyone!
Kyle Mercer:	Yes, but you need to observe the impact that it has. It's fine if it's got a positive impact, but if you observe the impact and really see it, I think it'll dissipate pretty quickly.
Karen Tolchin:	Right. The difference is when it comes from a place of authentic joy versus, "Gotta dance! Jazz hands!" That kind of frenetic place.
Kyle Mercer:	Authentic joy can even be a little understated.
Karen Tolchin:	Absolutely. I can feel myself growing considerably more understated, over the past year. By the way, Happy one-year coaching anniversary!
Kyle Mercer:	I feel like I've known you much longer than that.
Karen Tolchin:	I *wish* I had known you much longer than that.
Kyle Mercer:	There's a difference between showing love and being love. Part of it is egoic. I can hear it, too. There's this egoic quality of wanting to be seen as being so loving. This may be part of something that you need to heal. You've got a chip on your shoulder to prove how loving you are. Maybe Charlie's the vehicle so that you can show the world how loving you are.
Karen Tolchin:	Okay, because maybe there's a piece of me that thinks I don't have a good heart.
Kyle Mercer:	Yes.
Karen Tolchin:	That it's a performance.
Kyle Mercer:	It would make sense, even with your brother… It's like, always having to sacrifice yourself for

him or always be loving with him even when he was stealing all your attention. You have to prove how loving you are so that you'll be accepted. Do you feel any of that when I say it?

Give to yourself what you're trying to give to your children.

Karen Tolchin: Yes, absolutely. I've gotten attention and I've gotten praise since I was a little girl for being caring. I mean, it's even embedded in my name: "Karen."

Kyle Mercer: Oh, wow. I just heard that. Yeah. Then, that means that being so gushy and loving is an ego position. It's, "Look at how loving I am," and you need to let go of that.

Your child really shouldn't be the vehicle for you to prove to the world how loving you are. Love should set us free, not entrap us.

It's more you're just experiencing your love inside yourself. I think that this distinction between showing everybody how loving you are and experiencing your own love are two very different things.

Karen Tolchin: I agree. When it comes to self love, it's like, I have this impulse to leave the building. You're saying, "Stay in the building."

Kyle Mercer: That's right. Allow yourself to soak in your own love. Any love that you don't need to express is probably going to be real. There's a good percentage of the love that you feel you need to express that may not really be love.

Karen Tolchin: So, be more like Rainbow Rob. Be calm and loving of myself.

I like the litmus test you gave me earlier in this conversation. What effect is my love having on others?

Kyle Mercer: Yes, that's right. I think that is a great litmus test. You can really determine what's serving and what's not.

Bringing Stop Parenting Out Into the World

I've graduated from integrating Inquiry Method concepts here and there in my conversations with friends to explicitly promoting the **Stop Parenting** method to other parents. I have lunch with a dear friend. I tell her, "I'm so happy," and she says, "Oh my God, that's so different, so new. What's going on?" I say, "I'm writing. I'm writing around the clock. I'm annoyed with everything that's taking me away from writing. I'm totally inspired. I'm self-actualized. I'm living my bliss, here."

My friend says, "That's so great! Let's talk about **Stop Parenting**." I tell her how revolutionary I think all of this is, and then she asks for my help. I say, "Sure, lay it on me!" She said, "Well, my husband just got diagnosed with Type II diabetes. He's overweight. He has been for a long time and the doctor just determined that it's not being handled well enough. He actually has to go on insulin. At the same time, I'm noticing that my two children are both getting overweight, and I've struggled with weight my whole life."

At this point, I'd love to say that I used Inquiry with her to find out what was true for her, and then helped her use Inquiry with her family.

Here's what I did instead.

I said, "Oh my gosh, I just went to this great diet doctor and I've lost so many pounds, and I feel so energetic. Here are all the things that worked for me, and here's what you might consider doing. Maybe if you just completely overhaul your kitchen pantry and maybe if you change the culture in your household…" and then I just stopped myself. I thought, "Oh my God. What am I doing? My dear friend didn't ask me to share diet tips. She said she had a *parenting* question for me." Look at me. Teaching, guiding, shaping, molding. "I know exactly what's going to rescue your children and how you need to rescue and save your family!"

I took a deep breath and apologized to her. I said, "This shows how incredibly hard this **Stop Parenting** concept is for me. Here's what I think might be a mentally healthier approach. What do you feel is right for you? What if you sat down with your children and asked them what they think and feel about it, too? Tell them what's going on with their dad, and then ask them what they might want to do… Have a real conversation, and maybe try to collaborate with them. And please forget everything I said before."

I tell Kyle about it in our next conversation.

Kyle Mercer:	Sounds beautiful to me, but what do *you* feel about it?
Karen Tolchin:	Well, I feel ashamed of my first response, but honestly, maybe I've been beating myself up a little too much about it, because this *is* all new for me. I've been doing things one way for decades, and I've just given this one year, or less, so I think Rome wasn't built in a day and I probably need to stop using this as just another way to feel bad about myself.
Kyle Mercer:	Well, I think it was a victory because you noticed what you were doing and stopped it. I mean, that shows that the consciousness is in.
Karen Tolchin:	That's great! Well, to be sure that I really have integrated this knowledge, I had a special idea for this call. Do you recall that list from the very

	beginning of our book, the Top Ten List of Widely Held Beliefs about Parenting that I subscribed to before we started this project? I'd love to revisit it with you.
Kyle Mercer:	You got it.
Karen Tolchin:	I thought maybe we could do a little free association first, almost like call and response. I'll read each of the original items to you, and you tell me how you would revise it.
Kyle Mercer:	Okay, sure. Lay the old beliefs on me, and let's see what I do with them.
Karen Tolchin:	Perfect. Okay, Number One was, "Being a parent is the most important job you will ever have so you should do it as if your life and the lives of your children depend on it."
Kyle Mercer:	Here's my revision: "Your growth and self-care is the most important job you'll ever have. Your children and their well-being depend upon it."
Karen Tolchin:	Okay, here's Number Two. "Good parents are inextricably tied to their children on an emotional level."
Kyle Mercer:	I would say, "Emotional ties to our children handicap their ability to experience and grow from their feelings or emotions."
Karen Tolchin:	Number Three is, " Parents ought to show their children what kind of behavior works and doesn't work out in the world, because the world depends on parents to teach children how to behave."

Kyle Mercer:	"Children are a mirror for their parents. The most important way that parents teach their children is how they [the parents] behave in the world."
Karen Tolchin:	Number Four: "Left to their own devices, children will run amok."
Kyle Mercer:	"Our children naturally want to express creativity and joy. They naturally want to live abundant, free, healthy lives."
Karen Tolchin:	Number Five reads, "Children don't know what's best for them, so parents should actively correct, mold, shape and choose for their children."
Kyle Mercer:	"By using Inquiry with our children, we support them in knowing what's true for them."
Karen Tolchin:	Number Six is, "The world is full of dangers and protecting children from them should be a top priority."
Kyle Mercer:	"Protecting children from day-to-day problems interferes with their learning and capacity to become self-sufficient."
Karen Tolchin:	Number Seven is, "Parents should praise their children often to develop their self-esteem and should rush to intervene when their children feel bad."
Kyle Mercer:	"Praise teaches children that the authority on their self-worth is outside themselves. Inquiry allows them to self-determine their self-worth. At the same time, parents can create a safe place for their children to come to when they feel bad and have the skills to teach them to self-heal."
Karen Tolchin:	Number Eight says, "Parents should instill in their children a sense of respect, duty and family

	obligations, which is more important than personal desires."
Kyle Mercer:	"Parents who live in integrity and truth will be respected. Respect is inherent when we create boundaries for ourselves."
Karen Tolchin:	Number Nine reads, "It's possible to parent well, no matter what physical and emotional shape you might be in yourself. In fact, being exhausted, overweight and stressed out is probably a sign that you are a good, i.e. selfless parent."
Kyle Mercer:	"The most important lesson you're teaching your children is how you treat yourself."
Karen Tolchin:	Number Ten: "To see how well or how poorly someone has parented you have only to look at the child. The child is a walking advertisement for the parent."
Kyle Mercer:	"All children are unique. If you want to see how well somebody's parenting, look at the parent's well-being."

CONCLUSION

After a year of **Stop Parenting** conversations, it's time to return to my original questions:

1. Am I capable of **Stop Parenting**?

2. What are the (emotional/logistical) costs of practicing this method?

3. Do the benefits outweigh the costs?

4. If others are inspired to **Stop Parenting**, what first steps might they take?

First off, I'm surprised, happy, and relieved—you might even say gobsmacked—to report that yes, I am indeed capable of **Stop Parenting**. Using Kyle's litmus test—what's the parent's well-being like?—I'm parenting a whole lot better, and feeling a whole lot better, after my intensive year of coaching around parenting. As with most worthwhile pursuits, the program succeeds to the extent that I work the program. Luckily, life gives me daily opportunities to practice **Stop Parenting**.

I've come to see that every moment I spend with Charlie, I have a choice to make: either **Stop Parenting**, or keep parenting the old way. When I'm grounded and balanced, I pick **Stop Parenting**. When I'm not, I choose the old way—and regret it immediately. (See the Epilogue for concrete examples.)

Here's a brief accounting of the costs of **Stop Parenting** as I've experienced them.

Cost 1: My old identity. As a mom consumed with her son's well-being, my identity was completely entangled with Charlie's.

"How are you?" my friends would ask me. I would always answer with a Charlie Update. I was obsessed with Charlie's physical and emotional status. If he was well, I was well. If he wasn't, I inhabited his distress as if it were mine. My entanglement with my child was so profound, my own chest hurt every time he coughed.

Stop Parenting requires you to clean up those entanglements and replace them with intentional engagement. To do that, you must work to regain your own identity, not as a parent but as a person.

Cost 2: My social standing. That was next on the chopping block. My identity was all wrapped up in being Charlie's mom, so I received lots of support, sympathy, praise, and respect for my perceived selflessness. I had to let all of that go. At times, albeit not as often as I once feared, I have had to contend with a backlash of criticism, scorn, and even ridicule from certain family members, friends, and strangers. **Stop Parenting** has been hardest for me to practice in public, where strangers seem to have endless expectations for parents. The **Stop Parenting** approach has earned me a few withering looks and tart comments from strangers. Some were raised in a "Spare the Rod, Spoil the Child" environment while others are my contemporaries, especially Attachment Parenting devotees. **Stop Parenting** can look weird and wrong to parents up and down the spectrum.

It seems as if people have more judgments about parenting than anything else. It's funny how folks can work up a real lather about other people's parenting choices even (or perhaps especially) when they're struggling with their own parenting at home.

Cost 3: Old agreements with my child. I'd spent years teaching Charlie that he was my living, breathing heart. **Stop Parenting** required me to retrain my son to be his *own* living, breathing heart, for his benefit and mine as well. This was a process fraught with anxiety and suffering for us both. For me, entanglement meant love. That's what I'd been teaching Charlie through my behavior, and I had to stop.

Cost 4: All excuses for not getting my own house in order. I had turned my child into the perfect excuse to avoid what was out of balance in me, from my own physical and mental health to my beleaguered relationship with my husband. In essence, I had made myself so busy raising Charlie that I forgot to keep raising myself. **Stop Parenting** requires us to tend to our own gardens. There may be lots of scary stuff in there, like unresolved pain from childhood, or marital discord. Like me, your investment in your identity as a Super Parent has probably kept you too busy to clean it up. But here's the kicker: you can't effectively **Stop Parenting** until you do.

In case this list has made you want to run for the hills, let me assure you that, in my experience, the benefits of **Stop Parenting** far outweigh the costs. In fact, they're intrinsically linked to each one.

Benefit 1: Without your old pseudo identity as Super Parent, you get to discover who you are and what's true for you. **Stop Parenting** gives you permission to be an authentic human being and to grow those parts of yourself that you're interested in growing. Instead of living life mainly through your children (and suffocating them/stealing their lives in the process), you get to live your own life. As a parent—and as a person—you continue to take care of your child's basic needs and engage with him, but then only do what truly inspires you and has meaning for you. Your children get to find their own strength and take responsibility for their own lives. As a bonus, they get a parent who is genuinely happy, and not just one who is impersonating a happy mother for the neighbors while consuming large quantities of coffee and/or wine to survive.

Benefit 2: Getting scorned and criticized for my new approach by certain people taught me a valuable lesson: that I will survive without anyone else's approval, and so will my son. This is about your relationship with your child. Nobody else matters.

Once I got over my fear of a public shunning, I was surprised to discover that, for every raised eyebrow, I encounter five parents who are curious and open about my approach. When the goal is healthy, meaningful relationships with our children, the universe is rooting for us. Also, parents are pragmatic: if it works, they'll want in. Consider me Exhibit A.

Benefit 3: Trading entanglement for a healthy, loving engagement with my child was a total game changer. As my coaching dialogues with Kyle demonstrate, it was the toughest challenge for me. That must be why it's been immeasurably rewarding. My bond with Charlie is actually stronger than ever because he's getting to know his mother as a real person, not an archetype. At the same time, I'm getting to know who Charlie is because I've managed to stop fretting and attempting to exert control long enough to find out.

Contrary to my fears, Charlie has not suffered from my lack of helicoptering. He's been learning about his own strength. (Again, see the Epilogue for concrete examples.) We're actually spending more time together than ever, and that time is richer for its authenticity.

It recently occurred to me that most fairytales start with the death of a parent. That once struck me as barbaric, but now I see that children can't find their strength in the shadow of a parent. It's only after the parent recedes from view—preferably not through violence or loss, but rather out of respect for the child's autonomy—that the child utilizes his or her own resources, and learns that they're there. I've discovered that the best gift I can give my child is to take a giant step back, not forward.

As a side note, an old friend recently published a terrific novel called *The Nix* featuring a child who gets abandoned by his parent. The child's best friend reacts to the news by congratulating him on the opportunity to become a man. It's a shocking reaction, but it helps him much more than the typical sympathetic response ever could.

Benefit 4: My parenting challenges served as the inspiration for me to tend my own garden in a real and lasting fashion. If not for Charlie, I might have avoided the process altogether. After all, it required hard work, honesty, and more courage than I'm comfortable summoning on a daily basis. Now, I look at it as a huge gift: a deepening of my understanding of the world and my place in it.

When I'm tempted to rewrite an episode of my own childhood through my son, I just stop.

When I start to run the tapes of my late brother's life over Charlie's, and begin to act out of my fears for what havoc cystic fibrosis might wreak on us all, I just stop.

When I recognize that there's some hunger in me that I'm trying to fill through Charlie, I just stop and address the hunger directly.

When I find myself trying to engineer a certain kind of future for Charlie instead of living my own life and being a steady, grounded, and loving resource for him, I just stop.

In short, I've gotten much better at staying in my own lane. I'll always be there for my son, but his car, his road, and his journey are all his own.

I promised an answer to the following question: "If others are inspired to **Stop Parenting**, what first steps might they take?" The first and best step would be to check out the online resources associated with this book. Kyle and I are developing online resources including a list of suggested readings and a list of professionals who might help parents clean up their family entanglements and begin to engage with their kids in a healthy way.

This book stands as a living testament to the power of great coaching. I cannot recommend Kyle enough, but there are many paths to **Stop Parenting**.

We both wish you great meaning and joy in your own journey of discovery.

EPILOGUE

What follows are a few scenes from my adventures in **Stop Parenting**. Here's what it's looked like on the ground for me since the end of my year of intensive parenting dialogues with Kyle. I'll start with an epiphany involving Kyle, some merganser ducks, and a marooned kayak on a river in California. Then I'll share an epic **Stop Parenting** failure involving mermaids, Darth Maul, and an industrial glue gun. I'll show how I learned through my mother's death that the core wisdom of **Stop Parenting** isn't limited to my interactions with my son. Finally, I'll recount the small but significant strides I have made to **Stop Parenting**.

These scenes may leave you with the impression that **Stop Parenting** has been equal parts art and science for me. That would be absolutely correct.

One Wise Mother Duck

Exactly one year after the Mountain Experience retreat, I flew to Ashland, Oregon, for another retreat with Kyle Mercer. It was an "Inner Circle" retreat: free and open to all of Kyle's coaching clients, and less formal than the Mountain. Kyle offered to take us all river rafting just south of the Oregon border, on the Klamath River in California. I felt some anxiety about my lack of outdoor skills, having been raised by non-rafting folk, but I trusted that Kyle would never let any harm come to me.

"I feel like Bill Murray in *What About Bob?*," I told my fellow participants as I boarded the raft. "Mind if I tie myself to the mast?"

"No mast on a raft," Kyle said. "You'll be fine. Actually, you *are* fine. We all are. All is well."

There was some generalized hilarity around a new Inquiry Method motto the group was testing: "There is no hope; all is well." Someone fashioned a double hand gesture involving the "thumbs up" sign and a less socially acceptable finger.

While testing out a small inflatable "duckie" kayak apart from the group, I grounded myself on a rock. Marooned, I watched the rest of the group soar past me as I struggled to free myself.

"Is this some sort of spiritual test?" I shouted after Kyle.

"Hang on and we'll come back for you," Kyle called upriver.

I flashed him the new double-fingered Inquiry Method gesture and the other rafters laughed. My heart pounded. Was this like the "Death Therapy" scene in *What About Bob?*

My rescue from the rock took some time. I waited as two fellow rafters climbed up through the falls, bloodying their legs on rocks for me in a show of *bona fide* good Samaritanism. As I worked to calm my racing heart, I noticed a small, natural scene unfolding.

I might have been in turmoil, but it was calm, peaceful, and sun-dappled that day along the banks of the Klamath. A mother duck puttered along with eight ducklings pedaling behind her. She turned this way and that, possibly looking for food or shade. I noticed that she wasn't turning back to look at her ducklings. She trusted that they were all following her, and not getting sidetracked or possibly eaten by a fox. She pedaled forward, moving left and right, stopping and going, and the ducklings fell in line behind her every time. She was calm and casual, a model of maternal peace and groundedness.

At no point did the mother duck turn around and say to her kids, "Is everyone still present and accounted for? No one's been eaten by a fox? Great, well, I was thinking of turning right up ahead. Is everyone okay with right? Really? Nobody would prefer to go left? Because left would be fine, too."

By the time my inflatable "duckie" and I got freed from the rock, I realized that I've been one anxious mother duck. If Charlie had been following me in a river, we'd surely have gone in circles until we were both eaten.

"What kind of ducks are those?" I asked Kyle when I was safely back aboard his raft.

"Mergansers."

"Well, we should interview them for the book," I said. "They're total naturals at **Stop Parenting**."

"That they are," he agreed with a giant Kyle smile. Retreat mission accomplished.

Mermaids, Darth Maul, and an Industrial Glue Gun

Lately, I've found myself obsessed with mermaids. Not just mermaids, but a live action Australian TV show aimed at tween girls titled *Mako Mermaids*. I've binged all four seasons. Twice. I could say that I'm drawn to the nuanced writing, or the exceptional acting, or a certain nautical whimsy, but I'd be lying on all counts.

I found *Mako Mermaids* when I was looking for common TV ground with Charlie. Before he was born, I thought I'd be hand-milling all of his foods and keeping him away from all screens until adulthood, but CF changed all of that. In order to keep a small child still long enough for airway clearance treatments, movies and television programs help enormously. We watch something together twice a day. When he was an infant, it was Baby Einstein, which was perfect for us both: age appropriate for Charlie, and Zen for my sleep-deprived brain. But as Charlie grew and my faculties sharpened, the content started to matter more to us both.

The problem (as I imagined it) is that what engages Charlie usually involves light sabers, Legos, and action heroes. Not being a seven-year-old boy, I find all of those things mildly diverting at best.

Mako Mermaids worked for both of us for a long time because it had just enough action for Charlie: mer-men locked in battle over a magical, mystical trident. For me, there was a pod of mermaids who cast spells, sang songs to the moon, and had hair that looked fabulous even when it was full of kelp. Girls six to twelve are the target audience, but for some baffling reason, at the ripe age of forty-six, I was all in.

Sometimes, I watched even after Charlie had gone to bed.

Inspired by the show, I began to collect mermaid product at a rate you might call alarming. I was in denial about the weirdness of my *Mako Mermaids* obsession until Halloween, when I found myself locked in a stupid power struggle with Charlie over his costume. The bloom was decidedly off the rose for him regarding *Mako Mermaids*. He was all *Star Wars*, all the time, and he wanted to be Darth Maul for Halloween. For anyone who isn't living with a boy, Darth Maul is an evil Lord with a red face, yellow eyes, and a ring of stubby horns. (If Darth Maul worked at a local coffee shop, you would assume he had a long list of grievances about his parents.)

"When you say Darth Maul, don't you really mean Zach from *Mako Mermaids*?" I said. "I'll make you a trident with a giant moonstone."

"But I want a red light saber," Charlie said.

"Everyone will have a red light saber," I said. "You'll meet yourself coming and going. But NO ONE else will have a trident. Especially not one with a moonstone."

When Charlie paused to consider the trident, I took it as a green light.

For inspiration, I learned how to use Pinterest. I bought a hot glue gun—industrial grade. I dropped some serious coin at a craft store. I stayed up until midnight. Three nights in a row. And I made a glittering tail and seashell headband for myself using shells I'd collected on our weekly boating forays.

I let Charlie play with the trident two days early. By Halloween, what little charm it had ever held for him had evaporated.

On Halloween morning, Charlie said, "I want to be a skeleton."

I knew something was truly off-kilter when I found myself wondering if I could borrow another boy for trick-or-treating. Or a girl. Many of the girls at Charlie's school are gaga for *Mako Mermaids*. I know because we've debated its finer points in the halls.

"Nixie is my favorite mermaid," a nine-year-old will say.

"But wouldn't you rather have Mimi's talent for casting spells?" I'll argue. (I have strong opinions.)

Ever since I was a girl, my tastes have run to the super-girly, much to my mother's chagrin. She was a seventies feminist much like Hillary Clinton, equally proud that she never stayed home and baked cookies. She wrote ten books, one of them titled *Clout: Womanpower in Politics.* She kept waiting for me to ask for chemistry sets for Chanukah, but I never did. I wanted plastic junk stamped with rainbows and glitter, sewing machines, and Easybake ovens. (I was deep into Laura Ingalls Wilder, which explains why I look like a nineteenth century pioneer child in many of my elementary school photos.)

"A woman of your intellect," my mom would say, shaking her head. I gave her many occasions to say this. Like when she caught me watching *General Hospital* with our housekeeper. "Karen, a woman of your intellect..."

I was nine.

Mom never understood my yen for homemaking, much as I will likely never understand my son's bloodlust. How well do any of us understand why some narratives and symbols seize our imagination while others leave us cold?

The mermaid thing has me truly perplexed. I don't want to live in cold water, covered in scales. I wouldn't trade my legs and genitalia for a tail. And I'd probably lose all interest in singing songs to the moon after one night. But I cannot deny this fact: I love giving myself over to the realm of beautiful, fierce, and magical mermaids. Kind of like how Charlie loves Darth Maul and couldn't give a flying conch about mermaids.

I didn't fully recognize the Halloween Trident v. Light Saber Battle as the epic **Stop Parenting** failure that it was until after the candy had been eaten. The frenzied midnight hot glue gunning should have been a tip-off, but I ignored the clue.

Here's what I've come to understand. When I was a child, I didn't want a chemistry set, but my mother kept foisting one on me. Charlie never wanted a trident, but I foisted one on him. All the glitter in the world couldn't mask what I had done: I denied the essence of Charlie and asserted myself where I didn't belong. The more I fought him on his passion for the Dark Side of *Star Wars*, the more attached he would grow to it. If I didn't hurry up and **Stop Parenting**, Charlie might end up a forty-six-year-old man trying to get his kids to play *Star Wars* with him, all because his mother had a problem with Darth Maul.

The truth is that I'm not Charlie's playmate, I'm his mother. The chasm between *Star Wars* and *Mako Mermaids* is too large to bridge. More to the point, the divide separating childhood from adulthood, and children from parents, really isn't meant to be bridged. I've been controlling for happiness again, and the results are abysmal.

As penance, I decided to watch *Return of the Sith* once more with an open mind. I came away with some real wisdom—a lot more than a bunch of prancing fish-people had ever offered me. For the first time, I really listened to the Jedi Master Yoda as he counsels Anakin Skywalker, who is on the verge of losing his way and becoming Darth Vader. Anakin flirts with the Dark Side because of premonitions he's been having of his beloved wife's death in childbirth:

> **Yoda**: Careful you must be when sensing the future, Anakin. The fear of loss is a path to the Dark Side.

Anakin Skywalker: I won't let these visions come true, Master Yoda.

Yoda: Death is a natural part of life. Rejoice for those around you who transform into the Force. Mourn them do not. Miss them do not. Attachment leads to jealousy. The shadow of greed that is.

Anakin Skywalker: What must I do, Master Yoda?

Yoda: Train yourself to let go... of everything you fear to lose.

-IMDB.com

It was time to heed Yoda's warning. Like Anakin Skywalker, I was denying reality—the reality of my son and what interests him, along with the reality of the work I still need to do on myself. Through my stubborn attachment to a dream of perfect unity with my child, I was creating a nightmare for us both. Why hadn't it occurred to me that Charlie could dress up like Darth Maul for Halloween, and I could dress like a mermaid if I really felt like it, and nothing would be lost? Darth Maul might be doing some important psychological work for Charlie as he grows. He might be experimenting with male strength in all of its incarnations. The truth is that it's none of my business. Luckily, I have enough psychological work of my own to keep me plenty busy. There are still corners of my own garden in need of attention if I want to sow a different crop next October.

The stubborn hope for a perfect union and the fear of future loss are the two things that continue to trip me up. Never was this more obvious to me than when I attempted to parent my own mother on her deathbed.

"There is no hope; all is well"

When my mother was dying, I came to learn that my parenting impulses extend well beyond my relationship with my child. In fact, they can permeate all aspects of life, including work, love, friendships, and family relationships. During the four-year period my mom battled ovarian cancer, I struggled mightily with the same misguided impulses—trying to control situations, forcing togetherness and happiness, imposing my caring on others, and failing to calm myself enough to recognize what was true and respect others' autonomy. In the last six months of her life, my once-vibrant, happy, and engaged mother lost all interest in living. In the final stage of her disease, she couldn't eat more than a few spoonfuls of soft food at a time, and she suffered from perpetual nausea. Cancer seemed to have sucked all of the sweetness from her life.

"Every night before she goes to sleep," my dad told me, "she says, 'I hope God takes me tonight.'" He looked frayed to bits, watching his love of fifty-two years disintegrate one molecule at a time. "When she wakes up in the morning, she says, 'Damn it, I'm still here.'" I was surprised to hear a reference to God. When I told my mom that I was sure my brother Charlie was preparing an epic welcome party for her in heaven, she sighed and said, "I wish I believed that." It's not my brother she didn't trust; she couldn't envision the existence of heaven. Born in 1941, she was like many Jews raised in the immediate wake of the Holocaust: one quart low on faith. How do you continue to believe in a benevolent God after your community was nearly destroyed by genocide?

I tried to parent my father by giving him a break from caregiving. But as he put it, "I'm constitutionally incapable of leaving your mother, even for one night." At eighty-seven, he was baffled to be losing a wife almost thirteen years his junior, especially since my mother always embraced a healthy lifestyle. I was afraid that caring for her would kill him.

211

I tried to parent my mother by offering her some spiritual solace, but she had no taste for it or anything else. She had been the sort of person who flew to Berlin for a weekend, on a lark. Now, she had the air of somebody who had been mugged and couldn't get the authorities to do anything about it. I began to let myself get aggravated by her unwillingness to accept any solace from me or anyone else.

"I wish she would tell me how to help her," I said to my best friend Dean. "If you were dying, and I was there, you would tell me exactly what you wanted, right?"

"Absolutely," said Dean. "I'll tell you right now, just in case: I'd like handsome men milling about shirtless, and chocolate."

"Exactly," I say. "And if you were attending me, I would want those things, too—plus my family, a massage therapist, and some Native American drummers to help ease my transition into my new life as a blue whale."

But the truth was that my mother *did* ask for exactly what she wanted: death. When I called from Florida, she could speak only one or two sentences into the phone. One of them was always, "Can't you do anything to help me die?" The same thing happened when my brother Charlie was dying. He was thirty-four. It took me a decade to heal from the trauma of his death, but I understood that this was different. My mother was seventy-five, too fit and young in the 21st century to be felled by this fluke, but as she once put it with her trademark humor, "Nobody can say I'm going to die young." Her death was painful and primal, but I knew it wouldn't hobble me the way my brother's had. I was thirteen years older, with a son to keep me in the swim of life.

I tried to honor my mother's wishes and her experience of dying, but it was hard for me to resist the impulse to help, shape, and mold. Much of Kyle's parenting wisdom surfaced: "You need Charlie to show up for you in a particular way." I did the same thing with my mother, wishing she would show up and play her part in a particular way for me.

212

BRINGING STOP PARENTING OUT INTO THE WORLD

I raced between Florida and Washington, trying to meet a range of loved ones' needs as the newest spokeswoman for the Sandwich Generation. I scrubbed my parents' house clean to make myself useful, until my father pitched an epic fit because I tossed expired deli meat that had turned green into the garbage. I saw that the roles had reversed: I was playing the sensible adult who understood the link between rotten food and illness, while my exhausted father played the angry child. Yet I was chagrined to find that there was precious little I could do to parent either of my parents. Whether I was interacting with a child or a senior citizen, I was still stubbornly thinking of "parent" as an active verb.

I repeated one of Kyle's mantras to myself—"There's so much less to be done than we think"—and tried to be still and present with what was true. That lasted for five minutes. What was true was scary, dark, and out of my control, so I opened the escape hatch.

When there was nothing left to dust, I decided to digitize all fifteen of our family photo albums, scanning just under a thousand photographs. They had been languishing in a forgotten, hard-to access bookcase for several decades, and many of the yellowed plastic sheet protectors crumbled in my hands when I touched them. The quality of many of the photos was sketchy—aged to an orange tint, with the date scrawled in pen right across the images themselves—but I picked the hundred best shots and made my mother a Shutterfly book for Mother's Day. It spanned from her own birth announcement to a recent photograph of her grandson.

The last time I saw my mother give an authentic smile was two months earlier, in Charlie Jr.'s presence, when they were playing the card game "War." In another **Stop Parenting** failure, I fretted about the impact of so much parental absence on Charlie and brought him with me to D.C. as often as I could—more for me than for him. "War" was one of several ideas given to my mom by her friend Judy, a children's book author and thus a natural with kids. Judy gave her a formal tutorial one afternoon on how to relate to small children. In other words, I was raised by a woman who got curious about how to be an interesting playmate for a child only after she became a grandmother.

I finally stopped bringing Charlie with me when I saw how skeletal and listless my mom had become. When I walked into their home after a three-week hiatus in April, I was so shocked by her appearance that I worked hard not to burst into tears. It never occurred to me that expressing real grief would be just fine. "There is no hope; all is well."

My father and I were both amazed that she was still with us on Mother's Day, and I was grateful to be able to present her with the Shutterfly book. Thanks to JetBlue, I managed to divide a single Mother's Day between my mother and my son, a thousand miles apart. The Shutterfly book was too heavy for her to hold, so I knelt in front of her chair. We looked at her baby pictures, courtship photos with Dad, our trip to Egypt and Israel, and countless Cape Cod summers. As I turned the pages, I tried to read her face for signs that it was a pleasant experience for her. Was I doing it for her or for me? It was a classic **Stop Parenting** question.

"Who is that?" she asked, pointing to a photograph of a brown-haired toddler grinning on a Wellfleet beach, her arm around a slightly older boy.

"That's me, Mom." Her eyes widened, and then dimmed. This was a woman who published ten books on complicated political subjects—eight co-authored with my father—but multiple rounds of chemo had diminished her mind.

I was hungry to connect with her, this woman who somewhat randomly met a man standing next to a pile of cocktail shrimp at a New York party and therefore gave me life. Suddenly, I wasn't sure I really knew her, or that she really knew me. I wanted to have meaningful conversations, to share ardent declarations of love, to know all of her secrets—but she was already gone in all of the important ways. Even if she wasn't, that was never really her style.

My mother was reserved and private—loving but not effusive. When I forage my memories for proof that she loved me, the first image to surface is a yellow Post-It note. I used to receive clippings in the mail at least once a month from her. She'd read an article about a health issue or an academic topic I was researching, and she'd send it off with a simple yellow Post-It marked "Love, Mom" in her almost-indecipherable academic's scrawl. When I was in my twenties, I wished she would write me an actual letter and stick it in one of those envelopes. I mean, who communicates love with office supplies?

Now, I realize that every clipping represented a fervent hope for me, for my body's health, for the success of my career in Academe. Hope: before my **Stop Parenting** apprenticeship, it had always seemed like the cornerstone of a mother's love. If I'd kept every single yellow square of paper, I could blanket a significant stretch of the route I'd been taking from Naples to Washington. My mother's love might have been idiosyncratic, but it was steady, abundant, and true.

On the last day of her life, my mother was bedridden and short of breath. I held her hand for short intervals and said loving things to her. I was staying in a hotel a few blocks away, and a few minutes before 10:00 p.m., I started walking back to have a shower and take my own nightly meds when the home health aide called my cellphone.

"I think you'd better turn around," she said.

With her last breath, my mother expelled a granular black substance from her mouth, probably old blood from her stomach. I took the stairs two at a time and walked back into her bedroom to find the home health aide hastily trying to clean her face and hair. When he died, my brother spat out teaspoonfuls of something similar, a substance that looked like coffee grounds. Later, I asked my mother's physician about it. "Is there such a thing as the Coffee Grounds Stage of Death?" He replied with his trademark wit, "It was your mother's final commentary on ovarian cancer." I kissed her forehead, which was still warm, and told her I loved her.

"She waited for you to leave the room," the aide told me. "That happens more than you think."

That would be consistent with my mother's brand of love. She kept her death to herself, not to shut me out but to spare me. When I get quiet enough, I sense the truth: that we never needed to perform an elaborate deathbed scene of love between mother and daughter. We were two different people, but our love for each other was always there. It always would be.

At Last, Progress

Shortly after my mother's death, I go on the Inner Circle retreat in Oregon where I have my epiphany around the merganser ducks. I need this reminder because my relationship with my son has deteriorated.

"Charlie is the perfect barometer for how much you are in or out of balance," Kyle tells me, and I see that it's true. When I come unmoored and start to act anxious and needy, Charlie absorbs my energy and spits it right back at me. I start to see it as a gift.

Nobody needs my intensive mothering energies except me. My challenge is to turn my mothering impulse back on myself. There's one person who would benefit so much from a shower of my love and care and attention, and it's me.

In Oregon, I come to see that I haven't given myself nearly enough credit. I've grown considerably during my first year at Stop Parenting U (private enrollment, inaugural class of one). The philosophy no longer seems dangerous to me, or the practice unattainable. I am no longer desperate and inflamed. I might have setbacks, but I recognize them almost immediately and correct my course. I'm also far more coachable. I used to argue with Kyle all the time. Now I just listen for the truth in his observations and let it infuse me with a new perspective. He has an uncanny gift for hearing the truth no matter what story I spin. I'm deeply thankful that when he speaks, I'm able to listen.

The first time I become aware of acquiring some sort of mastery is in the car heading for a weekly boating foray one Sunday morning.

It's my favorite activity of the week, and I've built a shiny tower of hope around the possibility that Charlie will share my joy. I hope we get dolphins to leap in our wake, or that we discover a rare seashell. Something about my outsized enthusiasm triggers Charlie, and he starts to counterbalance me with a monologue in the "Let's Cut Off Everyone's Head/Fat Mama" genre.

I pull over and shift the car into park.

"Should I take you back home and leave you with a babysitter?" I ask Charlie in a low and steady voice.

"What?" he says.

"I want to have fun today, and this kind of conversation just isn't fun for me. If it's fun for you and you don't want to stop, that's fine—I'll just leave you at home while I go boating."

"You hate me!" Charlie screams.

"No," I say mildly, "that doesn't feel true to me. I love you. It would be fun to boat with you, but I would still have fun by myself, so you choose what you really want to do. Whatever you choose is okay. But I have no interest in that old kind of talk."

I realize that this isn't strategy on my part: I'm genuinely fine with either outcome. After years of urgently wanting a strong bond with my child, and trying to orchestrate perfect family togetherness, and caring deeply when things have gone sideways, this is new.

I wait calmly for Charlie to mull it over. After a minute, he says, "I want to go on the boat."

"I'm glad," I say. "Let's go have some fun." I pull back onto the road and catch his eye in the rearview mirror. We have a calm day on the boat, and while there are no dolphins, I feel more satisfied than I have in ages. And I realize it would have been equally nice if I'd had only my own company to enjoy.

I am utterly without agenda, and it feels fabulous. Major progress.

A few weeks later, I have what feels like another **Stop Parenting** success, again in the car. We are driving to school, and Charlie starts listing everyone he hates at school.

"I'm not interested in hating people," I tell him. I turn on the radio, and he starts to pitch a fit.

"What's wrong?" I ask him. "You sound angry."

"I AM angry!" Charlie says.

"Thank you for telling me that," I say. "Now, would you like to let go of your anger?"

"Yes!" he says.

"Sure!" I say. "Okay, close your eyes and feel where in your body the anger is."

"My toes!" he yells, kicking at the back of the seat in front of him.

"Okay, don't kick my car. The anger is in your toes. Now, imagine taking all that anger out of your toes and wrapping it around your heart like steel bands. Tell me when you've got it all wrapped around your heart."

"Done!" he yells.

"Great! Now take the deepest breath you ever took and burst those bands. Breathe it all out in a giant whoosh." I listen to him as he whooshes. "Is there any anger left?" He nods. "Great! Take another breath and whoosh some more." More whooshing.

I look in the rearview mirror. His red and squished up angry face has been replaced with a calm, almost beatific expression. He looks like a little mystic bathed in golden light. We hop out in the school parking lot, and he reaches for my hand.

Guided meditation has become a regular part of our morning commute, and it's lowered the intensity by a wide margin. This pleases me, but I try not to lean into it too much, or give it too much importance. I don't take it personally when he's out of sorts, and I do my best not to let him bring me there with him. Instead, I offer what I have learned.

He's welcome to take it or leave it.

A Stop Parenting Primer

1. Unlearning can be harder than learning.

2. The best parenting comes from a deep peace, calm, and presence, along with the lightest touch.

3. The knowledge we need comes from two sources: from within ourselves and our direct experience.

4. It's a totally flawed idea that we're born flawed.

5. There's nothing to be done except to love the child.

6. Let the world socialize the child.

7. Let children explore the world and be a safe place to come home to.

8. The whole message of this modern era of parenting is to override who somebody is.

9. We're stuck in our heads rather than in an organic engagement with the world.

10. We're all starving for a different way of being.

11. We think that if we trust a more authentic way of being in the world, then our kids are going to be out of control.

12. Stop Parenting puts the heart over the mind.

13. The rules for being in the world will come naturally to each of us.

14. The parental source loves us just the way we are.

15. I totally accept this individual just the way he is.

16. Rampant overparenting is creating narcissistic, self-important children.

17. Everyone is responsible for his or her own well-being.

18. The most destructive idea in western culture is that it's the parent's job to turn the child into something.

19. Most adults struggle with the belief that they're not good enough. This has a lot to do with the parenting they received.

20. If you think your parenting will shape your child's personality, how do you explain the radical differences between children in the same family?

21. Parental guilt comes directly from the idea that we're responsible for the outcomes of our child's life.

22. The most difficult issue that I have to work through with women is the judgment on themselves as bad mothers.

23. Most of us are carrying around negative energy stemming from the belief that we're a victim of the parenting we received.

24. I'm not advocating child abandonment; I'm talking about holding things in a different context.

25. The idea is to be very present with our children without controlling them. They want our attention and presence.

26. Some study showed that 95 percent of parent-child communication is corrective and only 5 percent is interactive; really, it needs to be the other way around.

27. To create a space of deep acceptance for our children, we must first do it for ourselves.

28. When business owners tell me they run their companies like a family, I say, "Oh no! Don't do that!"

29. Anybody demanding respect is completely out to lunch.

30. Let's not manipulate and control our children. Instead of being something to resist, let's be something to emulate.

31. You can tell how controlling you're being in a relationship by how much resistance you're encountering.

32. Setting boundaries for other people is control. Setting boundaries for yourself is self care.

33. "Tell the truth, but don't tell Grandma that she smells bad."

34. It's no wonder we're such unempowered, uninspired, unalive human beings, considering the conflicting messages we receive as children.

35. Children run the unspoken energy in the home.

36. Kids go through phases, and if you can't go grow through their phase with them, they're stuck with their phase.

37. Every child looks for a way to get a hook into his or her parent.

38. A child always wants to control the source of nourishment and the parent is the source of nourishment.

39. Get unhookable.

40. Parenting is the sweetest process of personal growth. It's not about the children growing: it's that they're forcing you to grow up.

41. "Tough love" is still totally hooked because the parent is triggered.

42. Wouldn't it be nice to have the wisdom to move gracefully and harmoniously through parenting?

43. The idea of good or bad parents is an egoic identity. I'm not a good parent or a bad parent; I'm just a being who has a child.

44. Here's what it really means to grow up. You have three choices in life: You either change it, you accept it, or you be unhappy.

45. Your children need your acceptance. Then you can either be happy or unhappy about what they're like.

46. A radical openness to what's true is even better than acceptance.

47. We have children so we can enjoy them, not serve them.

48. If you are happy and grounded in life, your kids will be, too.

49. How much of your parent's advice did you take?

50. If parenting worked, we'd all be enlightened.

51. We have an educational system that serves of the population well.

52. We feel schizophrenic when we get a conditional love message.

53. Ideally, all behavior would be corrected by someone other than the parents.

54. **Stop Parenting** is a self-actualization process. You can't do it without cleaning up your own baggage.

55. Your resistance is helping you find the untilled parts of your soul.

56. Your kids are going to turn out just like you, no matter what you say or do.

57. If you want your kids to be decent, be decent. If you want your kids to be happy people, be happy, but authentically happy.

58. Your child is imprinting for who you are, not what you say.

59. Let's throw out our definition of success as having a six-ty-hour job, seeing your children four hours a week, and teaching them that's the definition of success.

60. Being inauthentic with our children causes damage.

61. Let them have their own experience and be a safe place for them to come back to.

62. Use Inquiry rather than parenting to help children find their own truth about the world.

63. We have no authentic coming-of-age rituals anymore.

64. Muster the courage to let go of control. Hear what your child says and quit trying to manage him.

65. We're indoctrinating children into the cult of family. It's the same kind of brainwashing techniques that a cult would use.

66. As a life coach, I'm deprogramming people from the cult of family.

67. Traditional parenting is a form of criticism.

68. Traditional parenting isn't safe. It's an implied judgment that there's something wrong with you, that you have to be whipped into shape.

69. It's critical that we do our own spiritual work as parents. We need to parent our children from a place of wholeness.

70. Give to yourself what you're trying to give to your children.

71. End the hypocrisy of parenting.

72. Stop thinking you're a better judge of what your children need than they are.

73. Parents are a huge hindrance to our educational process.

74. Even trying to control for happiness is wrong. You're allowed to have your own happiness, but to foist it on others is an intrusion.

75. Every time we decide to intervene, we do some damage to the relationship.

76. Is the way you're loving creating more happiness in the person you're loving? If not, then it's not love.